ISBN 978-1-330-17106-6
PIBN 10043719

1 MONTH OF
FREE
READING

at
www.ForgottenBooks.com

By purchasing this book you are eligible for one month membership to ForgottenBooks.com, giving you unlimited access to our entire collection of over 700,000 titles via our web site and mobile apps.

To claim your free month visit:

English
Français
Deutsche
Italiano
Español
Português

www.forgottenbooks.com

Mythology Photography **Fiction**
Fishing Christianity **Art** Cooking
Essays Buddhism Freemasonry
Medicine **Biology** Music **Ancient
Egypt** Evolution Carpentry Physics
Dance Geology **Mathematics** Fitness
Shakespeare **Folklore** Yoga Marketing
Confidence Immortality Biographies
Poetry **Psychology** Witchcraft
Electronics Chemistry History **Law**
Accounting **Philosophy** Anthropology
Alchemy Drama Quantum Mechanics
Atheism Sexual Health **Ancient History**
Entrepreneurship Languages Sport
Paleontology Needlework Islam
Metaphysics Investment Archaeology
Parenting Statistics Criminology
Motivational

FULFILMENT

OF

SCRIPTURE PROPHECY,

AS EXHIBITED IN

ANCIENT HISTORY AND MODERN TRAVELS.

BY STEPHEN B. WICKENS.

The study of prophecy identifies in the mind the God of revelation with the God of nature and of history; and, if investigated in a right spirit of seriousness, may be mightily instrumental in establishing a strong and practical sense of religion in the heart of the inquirer.—*Chalmers.*

FIFTH THOUSAND.

New-York:

PUBLISHED BY LANE & SCOTT,

200 Mulberry-street.

JOSEPH LONGKING, PRINTER.

1852.

PREFACE

PROPHECY constitutes so large and important a part of divine revelation, that no apology can be needful for any attempt, however feeble, to elucidate its meaning, exhibit its fulfilment, and render the study of it interesting to the youthful reader.

Most works on the fulfilment of prophecy presuppose, on the part of their readers, a more extensive knowledge of sacred geography and general history than probably most of them possess; the writer of the following pages has therefore endeavoured to enliven his work by such an admixture of history and of descriptive geography, as he supposed would serve to render the subject intelligible and attractive to general readers. The information which it contains has been derived from the most authentic sources, and especially from the publications of those travellers whose researches have, within the last few years, thrown such a new and unexpected light upon the subject of Scripture prophecy.

In crediting quotations, he has usually, for brevity's sake, given only the *name* of the author; but by referring to the following list, the reader will generally find the *full title* of the work quoted, and, if it be a book of travels, the year in which the author performed his journey.

A Journey Southward from Damascus, in the year 1836. By C. J. Addison, Esq.

History of the Expedition of Alexander. By Arrian. Translated by J. Rooke.

Travels in Syria and the Holy Land in 1810–11. By J. L. Burckhardt.

History of Arabia, Ancient and Modern. By Andrew Crichton.

Travels in Greece, Egypt, and the Holy Land, in 1801. By E. D. Clarke, LL. D.

History of the Decline and Fall of the Ro man Empire. By Edward Gibbon.

Travels in the Holy Land, and other places mentioned in Scripture, in 1832–3. By Rev. R. S. HARDY.

Historical Researches into the Politics, Intercourse, and Trade of the Principal Nations of Antiquity. By A. H. L. HEEREN, Professor of History in the University of Gottingen.

Christian Researches in Syria and Palestine, in 1823. By Rev. W. JOWETT.

Narrative of a Journey from India to England, in 1824. By GEORGE KEPPEL.

Letters on Egypt, Edom, and the Holy Land, in 1836. By Lord LINDSAY.

Travels from Aleppo to Jerusalem, in 1696. By HENRY MAUNDRELL.

Dissertations on the Prophecies. By THOMAS NEWTON, D. D., Bishop of Bristol.

Travels in Georgia, Persia, Armenia, and Ancient Babylonia, in 1817–20. By Sir ROBERT KER PORTER.

Travels in Palestine and Syria, in the year 1830. By GEORGE ROBINSON.

The PICTORIAL BIBLE, being the Old and New Testaments, illustrated, &c. To which are added original notes, explanatory of the history, geography, natural history, and antiquities of the sacred Scriptures. Three volumes, Imp. 8vo.

This treasury of Scripture illustration was published in London, in 1838, and at once became a standard work. From a recent London journal we learn that "Mr. John Kitto, the author of it, when a boy of eleven years, had his organs of hearing destroyed by a fall from the roof of a house. But notwithstanding this, he has travelled extensively, and resided for some time in Bagdad, during a period when plague, flood, famine, and war were desolating that unhappy city. It was during his sojourn in the East, that Mr. Kitto, in despite of the disadvantages under which he labours, accumulated that store of knowledge, observation, and *comparison* which has rendered his commentary on the Bible so novel and valuable." On the subject of *Prophecy*, his literary researches, as well as his personal acquaintance with several of the places referred to by the prophets, have enabled him to point out some circumstances which previous writers had overlooked.

Narrative of a Journey to the Site of Babylon, in 1811; and a Memoir on the Ruins of Babylon. By C. J. RICH, the East India Company's Resident at Bagdad.

Narrative of a Residence in Koordistan, and on the Site of Nineveh, in 1820. By the same author

Travels along the Mediterranean and Parts Adjacent, in 1816–18. By ROBERT RICHARDSON, M. D.

A Relation of a Iourney begun An. Dom. 1610. Fovre Bookes. Containing a Description of the Turkish Empire, of Ægypt, of the Holy Land, of the Remote parts of Italy, and Ilands adioyning. By GEORGE SANDYS. Third edition, London, 1632.

Travels and Observations relating to several parts of Barbary and the Levant, in 1722. By THOMAS SHAW, D. D.

Travels through Syria and Egypt, in the years 1783, 4, 5. By M. C. F. VOLNEY.

Mr. Keith has well remarked, that Volney, "from the manner in which he generalizes his observations, and marks the peculiar features of the different districts of Syria, with greater acuteness and perspicuity than any other traveller whatever, is, although 'he meant not so, neither did his heart think so,' the ever-ready purveyor of evidence in all the cases which came within the range of his topographical description of the wide field of prophecy,— while, at the same time, from his known, open, and zealous hostility to the Christian religion, his testimony is alike decisive and unquestionable."

Narrative of a Voyage along the Shores of the Mediterranean, including a Visit to Egypt, Palestine, etc. By W. R. WILDE, M. R. I. A.

To originality, either of matter or manner, the present work makes but little pretension; and should it answer the end for which it is designed, the writer claims no other merit than that of diligence in collecting, and judgment in arranging, the materials of which it is composed. S. B. W.

New-York, April 1, 1841.

———

In preparing the work for a new edition, the whole has been carefully revised: some new matter has also been introduced, drawn from the following authorities :—

Biblical Researches in Palestine, Mount Sinai, and Arabia Petrea: a Journal of Travels in 1838. By Edward Robinson, D. D.

Travels in Egypt, Arabia Petrea, and the Holy Land. By Rev. Stephen Olin, D. D.

Neither of the above works were published until after the appearance of the first edition of this volume. S. B. W.

CONTENTS.

———

FULFILMENT

OF

SCRIPTURE PROPHECY.

CHAPTER I.

INTRODUCTORY OBSERVATIONS.

Propnecy defined—Large portion of Scripture consists of prophecy—Extent and subjects of Scripture prophecy—Christ the grand
theme of prophecy—The prophets—Different modes in which God
communicated his will to them—Manner in which they published
their predictions—Style of the prophetic writings—Prophecy an
emanation of the divine goodness—The prophetic denunciations
always conditional—Fulfilment of prophecy proves the inspiration
of Scripture—Infidel objection—Contrast between Scripture prophecy and heathen oracles—Use of unfulfilled prophecy—Succession of Scripture prophecy—Object of the present work.

By the word PROPHECY we understand the
foretelling of future events—the declaration beforehand of "things that shall be hereafter:"
not such things, however, as may be conjectur-
ed by human sagacity, or expected from the regular operations of nature, but such as can be
foreseen by none but the omniscient God, and
foretold by those only to whom the "Father of
lights" shall reveal them. Man, by the use of
history, may acquire some information respect-

ing the things that are past; but he " knows not what shall be on the morrow :" prophecy, so far as it goes, draws aside the veil which hides coming events, and lays open the scenes of the future.*

Every reader of the Bible must have observed how large a portion of the inspired volume is of a prophetical character. Scripture prophecy began to be uttered in Paradise, by our first parent, before the fall; " its parts are distributed over the various dispensations of religion for upward of four thousand years; and it ceased only with the last accents on the lips of the last of the apostles."

Thus extensive in the period of its delivery, prophecy is not less so in regard to the subjects which it embraces, and the period of time to which it refers. The fate of nations, and of individuals, the rise and fall of kingdoms, the succession of empires, the desolation of

---

* The words PROPHESY, PREDICT, and FORETEL, are precisely the same in meaning, but are derived from different languages. The word PROPHESY is of Greek origin, being composed of the two words πρό, *before*, and φημι, *I speak;* PREDICT is a compound of the two Latin words PRE, *before*, and DICO, *I speak;* the word FORETEL is, of course, formed by the union of the two English words *before* and *tell.*

mighty cities and countries, are among the objects of prophetic vision. It points to events near and remote, and embraces the most prominent and remarkable facts in the history of the world from its creation to the present day; while its unfulfilled predictions stretch forward to the period when it shall be declared that " time shall be no longer."

But the grand subject of Scripture prophecy was the progressive development of the person and kingdom of the promised Messiah— the Redeemer of the world. " *The testimony of Jesus,*" observes St. John in the Revelation, (xix, 10,) " *is the spirit of prophecy*"—the scope, design, and consummation of it. " *To him give all the prophets witness,*" (Acts x, 43,) is the language of another inspired apostle. They were chosen of God to testify beforehand, " the sufferings of Christ and the glory that should follow."

" Messiah's name attuned each lofty string,
   The world's Redeemer, and his people's King !
   HE in his glory, in his grief, appear'd
   The Star that led them, and the Sun that cheer'd.
   For him the kindling inspiration glow'd,
   And words of fire from lips terrestrial flow'd.
   Him, in his own supernal light they saw,
   And track'd his suffering path with trembling awe.

Beheld him conflict with the powers beneath,
Victorious burst the iron grasp of death,
A conqueror from the realms of hades rise,
And pass triumphant through the cleaving skies.
They view'd his empyreal throne sublime,
High raised o'er every realm of earth and time;
And hail'd that morn commenced whose cloudless sun
An everlasting course through changeless years shall
     run."—BULMER's *Messiah's Kingdom.*

Under the Old Testament dispensation, prophecy directed the eye of hope to a future Saviour, and was, as the apostle beautifully expresses it, " a light shining in a dark place," increasing in splendour and brightness, " until," at length, in " the fulness of time," the " day" of the gospel " dawned" on the world, " and the day-star arose" in the hearts of the faithful. As the *first* coming of Christ was the centre of Old Testament prophecy, so the leading design of the New Testament predictions is to confirm our faith in his *second* coming, and teach us to be " looking for and hastening unto the day of the Lord," 2 Peter iii, 12.

The catalogue of Scripture prophets embraces men from almost every rank and station in society. Among them were kings, princes, patriarchs, priests, and legislators. The greater part, however, were taken from the lower walks of life—husbandmen, shepherds, fishermen, &c.; but the office and the calling dignified the men. Their natural talents, education, and habits were as dissimilar as their occupations; but they all gave indubitable evidence that they were " moved" to the prophetic office " by the Holy Ghost."

Various means were employed by Jehovah in making known his will to the prophets. He " spake unto them," says the apostle, " in divers manners." The usual method seems to have been by the direct agency of the Holy Spirit, impressing upon the mind of the individual the message which he was to deliver. Sometimes predictions were delivered by the ministry of angels. Judges xiii, 2–5; Zech. i, 4; Luke i, 13. In some instances, as in the case of Abraham, and of Samuel, the word of the Lord came in an audible voice. Gen. xxii, 15–18; 1 Sam. iii, 1–14. Sometimes his determinations respecting the future were communicated in dreams, instances of which are recorded in Gen. xv, 12–16; xxvii, 12–15; and Jer. xxxi, 26. The dreams of Joseph, Pharoah, and Nebuchadnezzar, were also prophetic. At other times he made use of visions, which differed from dreams, in that they generally consisted of scenes and representations which appeared to a person when he was awake, and in possession of his natural powers and faculties. After the prophet had attentively considered the vision, its import and signification were usually made known to him. Ezekiel viii, ix, xxxvii; Daniel viii, x, xi. The book of Revelation, also, consists of a series of prophetic visions. Rev. i, 9, &c. " The method of communication which the Deity adopted in respect of Moses seems to have differed from all these : and whatever is to be understood by the phrase, ' The Lord spake unto Moses face to face, as a man speaketh to his friend,' (Exod. xxxiii, 11,) a superior kind of illumination is doubtless intended. It was the highest degree of inspiration."* But however various were the *methods* of communicating the divine will, they were always such as produced, in the mind of the person who received the communication, a conviction that it was from God, and enabled him to say, with confidence, " The *word of the Lord* came unto me."

When the prophets had received their message, they proceeded to publish it, which they did in various ways. Sometimes it was written out, and posted up where it might be read

* Collyer's Lectures on Scripture Prophecy.

by persons who passed by. Hab. ii, 2. When Jeremiah received the promise of Juaah's restoration from Babylon, he was commanded to " write the words in a book," (Jer. xxx, 2,) doubtless that, being placed in the hands of the people, it might be a source of consolation to them during the years of their captivity. But the more general method seems to have been that of proclaiming the predictions aloud in some public place ; thus Jeremiah was commanded by God to " stand in the gate of the Lord's house, and proclaim there" his word, Jer. vii, 2 ; at other times we find the same prophet publishing his message at the city gates, (xvii, 20,) and also at the gate of the king's house, (xxii, 1, 2 ;) and Jonah publicly declared in the streets of Nineveh the judgments of God against that city. Jonah iii, 4. Upon some important occasions, when it was necessary to rouse the fears of a disobedient nation and recall them to repentance, the prophets adopted extraordinary modes of expressing their convictions of impending wrath, and endeavoured to awaken the apprehensions of the people by the most striking illustration of threatened punishment. Thus Jeremiah made bonds and yokes, and put them upon his neck, to indicate the subjection to which Judea, and the neighbouring nations,

should be reduced by the king of Babylon. **Jer.**
xxvii, and **xxviii.** On another occasion, having
assembled the elders of the priests and people
and announced to them the judgments of Go
against Judah and Jerusalem, he took an earthe
bottle and dashed it to the earth, saying, " Eve
so will the Lord break this people and city, a
one breaketh a potter's vessel that cannot b
made whole again," Jer. xix, 11. So Isaia
"walked naked and barefoot," (Isa. xx, 2,) an
Ezekiel publicly removed his household stufl
from the city, (Ezek. xii, 1–12,) more forcibly to
represent by these actions some correspondin
calamities which awaited nations obnoxious t
God's wrath; this symbolical method of ex
pressing important circumstances being not un
usual among eastern nations.

The greater part of the prophetic writing
are poetical, and, like all oriental poetry, highl
figurative, abounding in metaphors drawn fro
the manners and customs, climate, natural phe
nomena, &c., of eastern countries. Som
knowledge, therefore, of oriental customs an
forms of speech is often essential to a full un
derstanding of the literal meaning of a predic
tion. Of this some instances will occur in th
course of the present volume.

The purpose of God in the dispensation o

prophecy was one of pure and unmixed benevolence to mankind. From the primeval promise in paradise, to the last of the apocalyptic visions, " good will to man" breathes in every prediction. The redemption of the world by Jesus Christ, the future glory of the church, and the universal extension of the kingdom of the Messiah, were the leading subjects of Scripture prophecy, and the themes on which the prophets delighted to dwell. Many of their predictions, it is true, consist of denunciations against ungodly cities and nations; but even here " mercy and judgment met together;" the design of these threatenings was to " lead men to repentance," and however apparently positive the terms in which they are expressed, they were always understood to be conditional; their execution depending upon the effect which they might produce on those to whom they were addressed. This we learn from the testimony of God himself, as given in Jer. xviii, 7, 8, where he says, " At what instant I shall speak concerning a nation, and concerning a kingdom, to pluck up, and to pull down, and to destroy it; if that nation, against whom I have pronounced, turn from their evil, I will repent of the evil that I thought to do unto them." Thus, when " the men of Nineveh repented at the preaching of Jonah," the Lord "repented of the evil that he said he would do unto them, and he did it not," Jonah iii, 10; and because Ahab humbled himself before the Lord, the execution of the divine judgments against his house was suspended until after his death. 1 Kings xxi, 29.

One of the benefits derived from prophecy, is the conclusive and irresistible evidence which it affords of the truth of divine revelation. "There is a voice which comes to us from the desolate sites where Babylon and Nineveh once stood in splendour, and reigned in power—from the prostrate condition of fallen Egypt—from the wonderful annals and remarkable preservation of the Jewish nation—from the desolation of Judea and the surrounding countries"—testifying that God himself was the instucter of the prophets, and that through his inspiration they declared in the beginning what should come to pass in the latter days. The foreknowledge of future events is one of the strongest proofs that can be given of a supernatural communication with the Deity. It manifests, in an equal degree with miracles, the interposition of a divine agency. It is as impossible for man, who "knoweth not what a day may bring forth," to predict the events which shall occur a hundred years hence, as it is for him with the word of his mouth to heal the sick or raise the dead. "The voice of Omnipotence alone can perform the latter,—the voice of Omniscience alone can reveal the former,—and both are alike the voice of God."

In one particular, indeed, the evidence of prophecy is more forcible than that of miracles; for while the proof from miracles loses something of the vividness of its effect (though none of its authority) from the distance of time, the force of the argument from prophecy is increased from that very cause. It is a *growing* evidence, gathering strength by length of time, and affording from age to age, as its predictions are gradually fulfilling, fresh proofs of its divine origin. "As a majestic river expands itself more and more the further it removes from its source, so prophecy, issuing from the first promise in paradise as its fountain head, acquired additional strength and fulness as it rolled along, and will still go on increasing in extent and grandeur, until it shall finally lose itself in the ocean of eternity."*

The opponents of Scripture have attempted to invalidate the evidence of divine inspiration

* Sir William Jones.

arising from prophecy, by alleging that the pagan nations of antiquity had their prophets and oracles as well as the Hebrews. It is true that they had numberless *pretenders* to the gift of prophecy. Their history abounds with stories and predictions of augurs and oracles ; and because it is known that these were the offspring of fraud and cunning on the one hand, and of ignorance and superstition on the other, infidels have affected to believe that all predictions of futurity are founded on the same basis, and therefore reject the prophecies of Scripture. It is, however, an easy matter to show the perfect contrast which exists between those contemptible mockeries of divine omniscience, and the sublime and holy predictions contained in the Bible.

The ancient heathen, when about to make war, or settle a colony, or undertake any event of importance, consulted their gods in order to ascertain their prospects of success. One mode of obtaining the desired information was by the observance of omens, which were interpreted by persons called augurs or soothsayers. Thus the most important events of state, as well as the concerns of private individuals, would often depend upon the direction in which birds might happen to fly, the greediness of chickens in devouring their food, accidental rencounters, words spoken by chance, and afterward interpreted into good or bad omens, eclipses, comets, unforeseen accidents, with an infinity of chimeras of like nature.*

But their most esteemed method of determining future events was by answers from oracles, or gods who were supposed to reside in particular places, and to reveal, through their attending priests, the secrets of the future to those who consulted them. There are said to have been about three hundred of these oracles in different parts of the world; but the principal ones were in Greece. They were generally located in the recesses of some thick wood or dark cavern, or in the secret places of temples. The most distinguished of them was the oracle of Apollo, at Delphi, which was consulted in cases of importance by most of the princes of the times in which it flourished. The oracles were accessible only at stated periods; and whoever consulted them was required to make large presents to the god before he could obtain the information he desired. Numerous ceremonies were also to be performed, and sacrifices to be offered, and, in case the omens were unfavourable, no answer was given. As

* Rollin's Ancient History.

the priests were themselves the sole judges of the omens, it was easy for them to evade every question respecting which it might be inexpedient for them to commit themselves. When, at length, the answer was pronounced, it was often couched in such obscure and doubtful terms, that it needed another oracle to explain its meaning. Sometimes it was expressed in so artful and ambiguous a manner, that it was capable of two opposite interpretations, and, therefore, however the event turned out, the credit of the oracle was sustained. For this the Delphian oracle was notorious. History relates, that when Crœsus, after presenting a most munificent donation, consulted this oracle in relation to his intended invasion of Persia, he received this reply :—

Κροισος Ἀλυν διαβὰς μεγάλην ἀρχην καταλύσει.

Crœsus, crossing the Halys, shall destroy a great empire.

This he naturally understood to mean that he should destroy the *Persian* empire, and, on the strength of this prediction, he commenced a war which terminated in the loss of his own. When, after his defeat, he reproached the oracle with having deceived him by a false prediction, he was told that the oracle had only declared that a great empire should be destroyed, and that he ought to have made a second inquiry to ascertain whether his own or the Persian empire was intended. By this evasion, the juggling priests saved the credit of their oracle, and the unfortunate king found he had been outwitted. When Pyrrhus inquired of the oracle what would be the issue of his war with Rome, he received a response in Latin, so " cunningly devised," that it might, with equal propriety, be rendered, *Pyrrhus shall conquer the Romans*, or, *The Romans shall conquer Pyrrhus*. Whenever they gave a more direct answer, and the event did not happen to correspond thereto, they accounted for the failure by pretending that some of the initiatory ceremonies had not been rightly performed, or that the gods were unfavourable to the person who made the inquiry.

The servility and corruption of the pagan oracles were notorious. Through intimidation, or bribery, they were frequently induced by public men to give such answers as would promote their own schemes. " Demosthenes, in one of his speeches to the Athenians, publicly charged the Delphic oracle with being gained over to the interests of King Philip; and the Greek historians give other instances in which it had been corrupted by money, and the prophetess sometimes deposed for bribery, and sometimes for lewdness."*

" The pagan oracles uttered no spontaneous predictions; unless a direct appeal was made to them, they observed a prudent silence. In saying nothing, they exposed themselves to no detection; and when they did speak, it was always with sufficient precaution."† None of their predictions went deep into futurity. They relate chiefly to the termination of affairs then actually in hand, the preparatory circumstances of which were well known, and the issue speedily to be determined. There was not even the pretence of foresight beyond a few years. Being thus consulted only in matters of immediate emergency, the result of which could often be foreseen by persons of ordinary sagacity, it is not surprising that the event should sometimes accord with their predictions. This served for a long series of years to keep up their credit; but at length their numerous frauds and impostures began to open the eyes of the more sagacious heathen, some of whom openly ridiculed their pretensions, and held them in utter contempt. They continued, however, to maintain their influence over the multitude until after the time of Christ, when, as the light

* Watson's Institutes.   † Horne's Introduction.

of the gospel gradually dispelled the darkness in which the heathen world was enveloped, the oracles fell into disrepute, and at last entirely ceased.

From this pitiful scene of juggling and imposture, let us now turn to the prophets of the Bible. We find these imposing no bewildering ceremonies on those who consulted them, and seeking no concealment in the delivery of their predictions. Their prophecies were not oracular responses " spoken in secret, in a dark place of the earth," but were publicly proclaimed in the most frequented places—in the courts of the temple, in the streets of cities, in the assemblies of the elders—and were afterward generally committed to writing, so that they might be " known and read of all men."

While the priests of paganism " taught for hire, and the prophets thereof divined for money," driving a gainful trade, and communicating their oracles only upon the inducement of large gifts, the prophets of the Lord, on the contrary, were distinguished for their incorruptible integrity. Even Balaam, who, we are told, " loved the wages of unrighteousness," while under the influence of divine inspiration could say, " Though Balak should give me his house full of silver and gold, I cannot go beyond the word of the Lord my God," Num. xxii, 18; and his subsequent conduct evinced the sincerity of his declaration. Num. xxv, 11–13.

As they were not to be corrupted by bribery, so neither could they be influenced by fear or intimidation. Their office frequently compelled them to deliver the most unwelcome messages under the most trying circumstances. They were often required to denounce the judgments of the Almighty against a rebellious people, and rebuke the iniquities of those who were exalted in rank and encircled with power. But "they concealed no truth which they were commissioned to declare, however displeasing to their nation, or hazardous to themselves." Yea, they "stood before kings," and boldly reproved them for their sins. Their fearless integrity often exposed them to "bonds and imprisonment," and sometimes even to death itself. "Thou that killest the prophets, and stonest them that are sent unto thee," was the reproach addressed to Jerusalem by our Lord. Matt. xxiii, 29–37.

In their predictions we discover neither artifice nor ambiguity. They had a clear, determinate, and consistent sense, and were spoken with all the confidence of truth, and generally with the plainness of history. Although a veil of obscurity hung over some of the prophecies which referred to distant events, until their accomplishment enabled men to "understand the interpretation," yet even these were never delusive in their character, or capable of double and contrary significations.

While the pagan oracles "hardly dared to assume the prophetic character in its full force, but stood trembling, as it were, on the brink of futurity, conscious of their inability to venture beyond the depth of human conjecture,"* the genuine prophets of the Almighty "looked through the course of succeeding ages, and proved, by the very sweep and compass of their predictions, that they were under the inspiration of Him to whom ' a day is as a thousand years, and a thousand years as one day.' "† They beheld with a clear and steadfast eye, and declared with authority and confidence, events so distant, so contingent, and at the time of their prediction so improbable, that no human foresight could have anticipated them. "Their prenunciations of the state of various people,—as the Jews, and the Arabians, and the Egyptians,—delivered thousands of years ago, offer, at the present moment, the most

* Bp. Watson's Apology.   † Watson's Institutes.

striking graphic delineation of these people as they actually are. Their picturesque represent-ations of the fate of ancient cities—the fisher-men that dry their nets on the rocks and rubbish of Tyre, the doleful creatures that nestle in the ruins of Babylon and Nineveh—give, with all the accuracy of a Flemish picture, the vivid re-alities of their present situation."*

In the subjects of their predictions the Hebrew prophets are inconceivably superior to the ora-cles of paganism. The predictions of the lat-ter were altogether destitute of dignity and importance,—the mere guesses of fortune-tel-lers at the issue of matters of local, personal, and temporal concern,—having no higher object in view than to promote the worldly schemes, and gratify the vain curiosity of kings and princes. The prophecies of Scripture, on the contrary, embrace subjects of the highest im-portance to the present and eternal welfare, not only of individuals and nations, but of the whole human race, and are inseparably connected with the religious hopes and expectations of mankind.

Their prophecies formed but a small part of the public instructions of the prophets; they also taught the people all the practical parts of

* Chalmer's Evidences.

a divine religion; they proclaimed the being and providence of God; they upheld religion and piety in the worst times, and at the greatest hazards; they exposed the pretensions of the pagan deities; they called men to repentance, conversion, and newness of heart; and they proffered the merciful promises of pardon and grace. In the midst of this course of doctrine, and in order to encourage the people to yield to it, they delivered their sacred oracles of a Saviour to come.[*]

The purity of their lives, the intrinsic excellence of their instructions, the disinterested zeal, and undaunted fortitude with which they discharged their ministry, the miraculous powers which they exercised, and the wonderful accomplishment of their predictions, fully demonstrate the claims of the Hebrew prophets to a divine commission, and prove that they were, what the Scriptures declare them to have been, " holy men of God, who spake as they were moved by the Holy Ghost," 2 Peter i, 21. " Can then the prophecies of Scripture be paralleled with the dark, venal, and delusive oracles of heathenism, without impiety ?" Who that has any knowledge of both, would for a moment think of seriously comparing the one

[*] Bishop Wilson's Evidences.

with the other, or pretend that they have equal claims to divine inspiration? "In the contrast, the interpreter of pagan oracles stands abashed before the prophet of the Lord, like the witch of Endor before the rising spirit of Samuel."[*]

While the fulfilment of prophecy thus establishes the divine authority of the Scriptures, the prophecies which yet remain to be accomplished answer even now an important end. They open our prospect into the future, encouraging us to put forth our utmost efforts, and to expect the accomplishment of our warmest wishes for the conversion of the world. While the mighty conflict between truth and error is still going on, we see how it will terminate, and know that the powers of darkness will at last be overthrown, and that, to use a prophetic phrase, "at even tide it shall be light."

> "Lo, radiant truth on high,
> With outstretch'd arm, the lamp of prophecy
> Hangs o'er a darken'd world,"

and the light which it affords has cheered the church in her darkest hours, and been her consolation and support in the most troublous times.

---

[*] Stowe's Introduction to the Study of the Bible.

" Long in this weary wilderness, the word
That speaks of happier scenes hath been her stay ;
And urging oft her rude and cheerless way
Through many a thorny brake, her tearful eyes
Have turn'd in holy transport to the skies,
And realized, by faith's transpiercing power,
The bliss of that anticipated hour,
When, glorious, seated on his conquering throne,
Messiah's sway a subject world shall own ;
When earth's wide realms Jehovah's praise shall sing,
And bow the suppliant knee to heaven's immortal King."

BULMER'S *Messiah's Kingdom.*

With a brief chronological view of the succession of Scripture prophets, mentioning the leading subjects of their prophecies, we will close the present chapter.

" The first man, ADAM, has an undoubted right to stand at the head of the prophets, as he does at the head of the human race. His declaration concerning marriage, ' *For this cause shall a man leave his father and mother, and cleave to his wife,*' is so truly *prophetic*, that no doubt can be formed on the subject. There was then nothing in nature or experience to justify such an assertion ; and he could have it only by divine inspiration. The millions of instances which have since occurred, and the numerous laws which have been founded on this principle among all the nations of the earth, show with what precision the declaration was con ceived, and with what truth it was published to the world."*

After the fall, guilty man was not thrust out of paradise till prophecy had whispered some hope of a future Saviour, in the promise that the "*Seed of the woman*" should "bruise the head of the serpent."

"ENOCH, the seventh from Adam," is called a prophet in Jude 14, 15, where a fragment of one of his prophecies is preserved.

NOAH, one hundred and twenty years before the deluge, was divinely premonished of that tremendous judgment; and previous to his death he delivered predictions respecting his sons.

ABRAHAM received prophetic annunciations of the "*Seed*" in whom "all the families of the earth should be blessed;" of the multiplication of his posterity, their affliction for four hundred years in a strange country, and their subsequent possession of the promised land.

ISAAC foretold the subjection of Esau's descendants to those of Jacob.

Instructed by the spirit of prophecy, "JACOB, when he was a dying," predicted the advent of "Shiloh," and told his sons what should befall their posterity in future days.

* Dr. A. Clarke.

JOSEPH was favoured with prophetic dreams himself, and had the gift of interpreting those of others; he also foretold the redemption of Israel from the bondage of Egypt.

After the exodus, prophecy rekindled its torch. MOSES, who was one of the most eminent of the prophets, predicted the coming of the Messiah, under the designation of *a prophet like unto himself*, and foretold some of the most remote events of the Jewish history. About the same time, also, the unwilling prophecies of BALAAM were delivered.

After the death of Moses there seems to have been a cessation of prophecy for about four hundred years. "The word of the Lord was precious in those days; there was no open vision," until the period when "SAMUEL was established to be a prophet" in Israel. 1 Sam. iii, 1, 20.

The age of prophecy, emphatically so called, now commenced. From this time to the close of the Old Testament, the succession of prophecy was uninterrupted. First came DAVID, and tuned his harp; mingling in his psalms devotion, poetry, and prophecy together. The succession was kept up by some seers of minor note, until the appearance of those remarkable prophets ELIJAH and ELISHA, whose histories form so prominent a part of the two books of Kings.

JONAH prophesied during the reign of Jeroboam II., king of Israel. AMOS, HOSEA, and MICAH, prophesied about the same time, or soon after, and denounced the judgments of God against the corruptions of Israel and Judah, and also against the inhabitants of Philistia, Edom, Ammon, and Moab.

Contemporary with these, also, was ISAIAH, the prince of the prophets, who continued until the time of Hezekiah, king of Judah. From the number, variety, and explicitness of his predictions concerning the advent, character, ministry, sufferings, and death of the Messiah, and the future glory of the church, Isaiah has, not unaptly, been denominated the evangelical prophet. He also testified against the crimes of the Jews, and declared the fate of Babylon, Philistia, Moab, Egypt, and Tyre.

NAHUM came next, bearing " the burden of Nineveh ;" then JOEL, whose prophecies relate principally to the Jews ; and ZEPHANIAH, who predicted also the punishment of Philistia, Moab, Ammon, and Nineveh.

HABBAKUK flourished in the reign of Jehoiakim, and foretold the captivity of Judah by the Chaldeans, as did also JEREMIAH, who lived to see the fulfilment of his prediction, and utter his *Lamentations* over the desolation of the holy city. He likewise foretold the termination of their captivity at the end of seventy years, and denounced the divine judgments upon several other nations.

EZEKIEL, who followed the Jews in their captivity, predicted the calamities which God, through the instrumentality of Nebuchadnezzar, would bring upon Judea and the surrounding countries. About this time, also, it is supposed that OBADIAH delivered his prophecy concerning the destruction of Edom.

In Babylon, DANIEL arose, and pointed out the succession of the four great empires of Assyria, Persia, Greece, and Rome. He likewise fixed the precise time of Messiah's appearance, and foretold the rise and fall of antichrist, and the universal prevalence of the true religion.

HAGGAI and ZECHARIAH returned with the Jews from Babylon; they reproved the languid nation for their delay in rebuilding the temple, encouraged them by promises of future prosperity, and delivered several predictions relative to the Messiah and his kingdom, and the future condition of the Jews.

MALACHI, the last of the Old Testament prophets, flourished in the days of Nehemiah. He

reproved the priests and people for their hypoc-
risy and general wickedness, and predicted the
coming of Christ, and of the "Messenger" who
should "prepare the way" before him.

"Here is a succession of divinely inspired
men, by whom God 'at sundry times and in
divers manners spake unto the fathers,' from
the beginning of the world down to the restoration from the Babylonish captivity, a period of
three thousand six hundred years."

A pause of four hundred years then elapsed,
during which every whisper of prophecy was
hushed, "until Christ our Lord arose—pre-
ceded, according to the prophetic declaration,
by his precursor—and predicted the destruction
of Jerusalem, and the dissolution of the Jewish
polity."

He was followed by St. PAUL, who prophesied the recovery of the Jews; and predicted the rise of the papal apostacy, under the
designation of "the man of sin—the son of
perdition," 2 Thessalonians ii, 3.   Last of all
came St. JOHN, who, in the prophetic visions
of the apocalypse, foreshows the most remarkable revolutions and events in the Christian
church from his own time until the final and
complete triumph of Christianity, and the per-
fecting of its glory in the heavenly world, when,

to use the apostle's own expression, " the mystery of God shall be finished." The revelations of the beloved disciple close the dispensation of prophecy, and the canon of Scripture together. " The vision is then shut up, the testimony is sealed, and the word of the Lord is ended."

" It is obvious that the wide range and prodigious extent of Scripture prophecy gives the subject an importance and sublimity, a sort of impress of divine magnificence, which, when verified by the respective fulfilments, surpasses all that we could have conceived. We have not merely one or two oracular declarations, but a whole system of prescient grandeur, running through all time, and stretching to the consummation of all things."*

The prophecies of Scripture may be divided into three classes.

1. Prophecies relating to the Jewish nation in particular.

2. Prophecies relating to other nations and empires.

3. Prophecies relating to the person and kingdom of the Messiah.

The majority of these predictions have al-

* Wilson's Evidences.

ready met their accomplishment ; some are at the present time in course of fulfilment, while others, as we have before observed, look forward to the far-distant future.

It is our purpose in the following pages to select some of the most striking and remarkable of those predictions which have been fulfilled, or now are fulfilling in the world, and trace their accomplishment in the history of the nations, and in the present state of the people and. countries to which they refer.   We shall then see how wonderfully " the history of the world has responded to the prophecies of the Bible, and echoed back to the ' holy men' who uttered them, a complete assurance that they ' spake as they were moved by the Holy Ghost.' "*

* M'Ilvaine's Lectures.

CHAPTER II.

PROPHECIES RESPECTING ISHMAEL'S POSTERITY.

The Arabs descended from Ishmael—Prophecies respecting Ishmael—Refer to his posterity rather than to himself—Hagar and Ishmael sent out from Abraham's family—Their sufferings and deliverance in the wilderness—Reflections—Ishmael lives an unsettled life—His sons the founders of twelve tribes—His posterity, according to the prophecy, become a "great nation"—They are a "wild" people—They retain the manners and customs of their ancestors—They live in a state of hostility with all other nations—Are robbers by profession—Manner in which they justify their robberies—Their hospitality—The Arabs have maintained a perpetual independence—Were never conquered by the Egyptians, Assyrians, or Persians—Alexander's projects against them defeated by his death—Were not subdued by the Romans—Do not acknowledge the authority of the Turks—Objections of Gibbon refuted by himself—Character of the Arabs, by Sandys—Testimony of Volney—Concluding reflections.

ONE of the promises made to Abraham, was, that he should be the " father of many nations." This promise was abundantly verified. Since the days of Noah and his sons there has been no man whose posterity is equally numerous, or to whom so many nations refer their origin. The most distinguished branches of his family are the Arabs and the Jews, the former the descendants of Ishmael, the latter of Isaac. Concerning each of these nations there are some remarkable prophecies, and both of them exist at the present day, separate and distinct from the rest of mankind, and from each other, a standing proof of the power and providence of God, and of the truth of divine revelation.

The principal prophecy concerning Ishmael and his posterity is contained in the language of the angel to Hagar, when she fled from the face of her mistress. "And the angel of the Lord found her in the wilderness, and said unto her, ' Return to thy mistress and submit thyself under her hands.' And the angel of the Lord said unto her, ' I will multiply thy seed exceedingly that it shall not be numbered for multitude. Behold, thou art with child, and shalt bear a son, and shalt call his name Ishmael; and he will be a wild man; his hand will be against every man, and every man's hand against him : and he shall dwell in the presence of all his brethren,'" Gen. xvi, 9–12. Some additional circumstances are contained in Genesis xvii, 20, where, in answer to Abraham's prayer, "O that Ishmael might live before thee !" Jehovah graciously assures him, "As for Ishmael, I have heard thee : behold, I have blessed him, and will make him fruitful, and will multiply him exceedingly : twelve princes shall he beget, ‸ l I will make him a great nation."

"The usual idiom of the Scripture requires us to understand in both passages what is said of Ishmael personally to be true also of his descendants. Indeed, it is rather his posterity than himself that is primarily intended. When it is said, ' I will multiply him exceedingly—I will make him a great nation,' the word ' him' obviously means his posterity ; for no one can imagine that he himself was meant to be multiplied in virtue of this promise, neither can one man be called a nation,—so, likewise, when it is said ' his hand shall be against every man, and every man's hand against him,' it is evident that one man could not subsist alone in open enmity to all the world, nor could one man's hand be literally against every man's. There is, moreover, not the slightest hint in Scripture, nor any reason to believe, that Ishmael lived personally in a state of opposition to his brethren. Throughout this whole prediction, therefore, Ishmael must be viewed as the representative of his posterity. What is declared of him, and promised to him, was intended to be affirmed of his descendants and fulfilled in them."*

For several years after his birth, Ishmael and his mother remained in the family of Abraham, and, until the fourteenth year of his age, he

* Bush's Notes on Genesis.

doubtless expected to be the sole heir of his father. At this period, however, the birth of Isaac, who was to be the heir of the promises, caused a great change in the condition of Ishmael, who, irritated probably at being superseded in the inheritance by his younger brother, appears to have treated him with rudeness and contempt. This did not escape the jealous eye of Sarah, who in consequence insisted on the immediate expulsion of Hagar and Ishmael from the family. Abraham, however, was loth to proceed to such extremities. His feelings were different from those of Sarah, who fixed her affections exclusively on Isaac, and regarded Ishmael as an intruder and a rival : but Abraham, as the father of both, felt a paternal affection toward each, and the course proposed by Sarah " was very grievous in his sight because of his son." It was however in accordance with the designs of God, and Abraham was directed to comply. In this, as in various other instances, the patriarch manifested his exemplary faith and obedience. It was painful to his feelings as a father to concur in so severe a measure ; but some gleam of futurity was afforded to enlighten the darksome but appointed path. " And God said unto Abraham, ' Let it not be grievous in thy sight because of the lad, and because of thy bond-woman : in all that Sarah hath said unto thee, hearken unto her voice ; for in Isaac shall thy seed be called. And also of the son of the bondwoman will I make a nation, because he is thy seed,'" Gen. xxi, 12.

With a small supply of provisions and a bottle of water, Hagar, with her son, who was now about sixteen or seventeen years old, was sent forth to find a home in some of the surrounding districts. Directing her steps toward her native country, she wandered with the lad in the wilderness of Beersheba. In a few days the water is spent, and poor Hagar pants along the solitary desert, turning hither and thither in search of some scanty supply. Not a drop is to be found ; and at length, arriving at some shrubs, she sat down with her exhausted, and, as she supposed, *dying* son, beneath the welcome shade. Unable to witness his expiring agonies, she laid him under one of the shrubs and retired to a short distance ; "for she said, ' Let me not see the death of the child,' and she sat over against him, and lifted up her voice and wept," Gen. xxi, 16. Who can imagine the pangs of that excruciating moment, or the bitterness of the tears she shed ? A more finished picture of distress it would be difficult to conceive. Had there been any ear to hear, any eye to pity, or any hand to relieve the sufferers, their cries and tears might have been mingled with hope; but as far as human aid was concerned, their situation was apparently desperate, and however much we may blame, we can scarcely be surprised at Hagar's distrust of the promises made to her on a former occasion, when she saw that son who was to be the father of a great nation, ready to perish before her eyes. But God was not unmindful of his promises: at this critical moment an angel again appeared to the desponding mother, and directed her to a well of water close at hand, whence she replenished her bottle and supplied her fainting son. The wanderers then continued their journey as far as the wilderness of Paran, where they took up their residence.

"In this distressing circumstance in the life of Hagar, a superficial observer might see nothing but a curious concurrence of ordinary events. The insolence of Ishmael irritated the temper of Sarah; she procured his expulsion and that of his mother from her household; retiring in disgrace, she narrowly escaped destruction in the wilderness, and afterward took up a casual residence in the vicinity. But if we pay a proper attention to these events, we shall view them with another eye. Every circumstance was connected with a vast providential plan. The folly of Ishmael, the conduct of Sarah, the compliance of Abraham, the various occurrences connected with the settlement in Paran, concurred to accomplish the predestined purposes of Jehovah;"* for God does not always, nor even generally, bring his predictions to pass by miraculous means, but by the operation and concurrence of natural causes. Ishmael, in consequence of his expulsion from his father's house, and the way of life into which he was thus forced, became early inured to hardships ; and his freedom from restraint, and the habit of reliance on himself which his mode of life must have induced, did much to foster that love of liberty and independence of character which was ascribed to him by the prophecy, before his birth.

"He dwelt in the wilderness of Paran, and became an archer," Gen. xxi, 20. "The expression, ' he became an archer,' " observes Professor Bush, " unquestionably denotes warlike character and practices. It is but another mode of saying that he began to be distinguished for lawless and predatory habits, as his descendants have always been."

* Cox's Female Scripture Biography.

It was also specified that he should be the father of " twelve princes." In a subsequent part of the Mosaic history, we find a notice of the fulfilment of this prediction. Moses, when enumerating the immediate descendants of Ishmael, concludes his account in these words :— " These are the sons of Ishmael, and these are their names, by their towns, and by their castles ; twelve princes according to their nations;" by which we understand, not that Ishmael's twelve sons were independent sovereign princes, but that they became the heads or founders of so many distinct tribes,* in the same manner as the sons of Jacob were the heads of the twelve tribes of Israel. Of Ishmael's personal history we have no further knowledge, except that he joined with his brother Isaac in paying the last tribute of respect to his father, and that he died in the one hundred and thirty-seventh year of his age. Gen. xxv, 9, 18.

We have now seen the accomplishment of the prediction so far as Ishmael himself is concerned ; but, as was before observed, the pro-

* The Arabs of the present day are divided into separate tribes, the heads of which are commonly called *Emirs*, or princes.

phecy refers not so much to Ishmael personally, as to his posterity: we will, therefore, proceed to trace its fulfilment in the history and present state of the Arab tribes.

"*I will multiply him exceedingly—I will make him a great nation.*"—This prediction was fulfilled as soon as in the course of nature it could be accomplished. In process of time, the descendants of Ishmael became a " great nation," and such they have continued to the present day. They are mentioned in Scripture under the names of Ishmaelites, Hagarenes, and Arabians.

It must not be forgotten, however, that under the general name of Arabs many persons confound two distinct classes of people, who, though inhabiting the same countries, are of widely different characters. One class live in cities and towns, and subsist by agriculture and commerce ; the other class comprise the roving, pastoral tribes, who inhabit the desert and dwell in tents. The latter are the posterity of Ishmael, and are commonly distinguished from the other Arabs by the name of Bedouins.*

* The word Bedouin is a corruption of the Arabic *badwi*, which is derived from the substantive *badw*, " an open country, a desert," and signifies an inhabitant of the desert.

4

The numbers leading this wandering and precarious mode of life are incredible. They are not confined to the deserts of Arabia. "From the banks of the Indus on the east, to those of the Senegal on the west, are colonies of them to be met with; and between north and south, they are scattered from the Euphrates to the island of Madagascar. Of all nations they have spread themselves farthest over the world; the Tar-

of the globe."*

He will be a wild man.—The original signifies literally "a wild-ass-man,"† for the word which our translators have rendered "wild," is the same that is applied to the *onager*, or wild ass, in other parts of the Scriptures. The figure is very striking. The principal qualities of the wild ass are savage independence, prodigious swiftness, a disposition to assemble in troops, and a fondness for the wilderness; all which strongly characterize the descendants of Ishmael. The description of this animal in the book of Job will recur to the recollection of every student of the Bible.

* Niebuhr's Travels in Arabia.

† This form of expression is still used among the Arabs, who employ the term "wild ass," to designate a person of a contumacious, untractable disposition.

"Who hath sent out the wild ass free?
Or who hath loosed the bands of the wild ass?
Whose house I have made the wilderness,
And the barren land his dwellings.
He scorneth the multitude of the city,
Neither regardeth he the crying of the driver.
The range of the mountains is his pasture,
And he searcheth after every green thing."

Job xxxix, 5–8.

Nothing can be more descriptive than this of the wild, wandering, lawless lives of the Bedouin Arabs, whose descent from Ishmael is admitted by the learned, and gloried in by themselves. God himself has *sent them out free;* he has loosed them from all political restraint. The *wilderness* is their habitation, and in the *parched land,* where no other human beings could live, they *have their dwellings.* Claiming the barren plains of Arabia as their patrimonial domain, they have, from the days of their great ancestor, down to the present time, ranged the wide extent of the burning sands which separate them from all surrounding nations, as rude, savage, and untractable as the wild ass himself. *They scorn the city,* and therefore have no fixed habitation. " It is in the lonely wilderness and the rugged mountains that their attachments centre; because it is there that they can live without ceremony and without control. Their sterile sands are dearer to them than the spicy regions of the south, and they would consider the security of cities but a poor compensation for the loss of their independence. The tent* they regard as the nursery

* The common Arab tent is of an oblong figure, varying in size according to the wants or rank of the owner. A length of from twenty-five to thirty feet, by a depth or breadth not exceeding ten feet, form the dimensions of a rather large family tent. The height of the centre poles, which are made higher than the others, in order to give a slope to throw off the rain, varies from seven to ten feet; but the height of the side posts seldom exceeds five or six feet. The covering of the tent is usually black goat's hair, so compactly woven as to be impervious to the heaviest rain; but the side coverings are often of coarse wool. The front of the tent is usually kept open, except in winter. The interior is divided into two apartments by a curtain hung up against the middle poles of the tent. One of these apartments is for the men, and one for the women. Sometimes there is a third apartment for the cattle

of every noble quality, and the desert as the only residence worthy of men who aspire to be the unfettered masters of their own actions. They cannot imagine how existence can be endured, much less enjoyed, except in a dwelling of goat's hair which they can pitch and remove at pleasure."* They may be said to have no lands, and yet *the range of the mountains is their pasture;* they pitch their tents and feed their flocks wherever they please; and they *search after every green thing*—are continually looking after prey, and seize on every kind of property that comes within their reach.

" Even in the ordinary sense of the epithet ' wild,' " observes the editor of the Pictorial Bible, " there is no other people to whom it can be applied with more propriety than to the Arabs, whether used in reference to their character, mode of life, or place of habitation. We have seen something of the Arabs and their life, and always, we felt the word *wild* to be precisely that by which we should choose to characterize them. Their chosen dwelling place is the inhospitable desert, which offers no attractions to other eyes, but which is all the dearer to them for that desolation, inasmuch as it secures to them that independence and unfetter-

* Chricton.

ed liberty of action which constitute the charm of their existence, and which render the minute boundaries and demarcations of settled districts, and the restraints and limitations of towns and cities perfectly hateful in their sight. The simplicity of their tented habitations, their dress, and their diet, we can also characterize by no more fitting epithet than ' wild ;' and that epithet claims a still more definite application when we come to examine their continual wan derings with their flocks and herds, their constant readiness for action, and their frequent predatory excursions against strangers or against each other."

Except in the article of religion, their manners and customs have suffered little or no change during the long period of upward of three thousand years. Their manner of living, in many respects, forms a perfect picture of primitive usages, as described by the sacred writers. Coming among them we can hardly help fancying ourselves carried back to the ages which immediately succeeded the flood. " The forms we see present us the picture of the old patriarchs with scarcely a single alteration. We may listen to their language, number their possessions, partake of their food, examine their dress, enter their tents, attend the ceremonies of their marriage festivals, and present ourselves before the prince, still all is the same. At the well they water their flocks; they sit at the door of their tents in the cool of the day; they take 'butter, and milk, and the calf which they have dressed,' and set it before the stranger; they move onward to some distant place, and pitch their tent near richer pasturage; and all the treasures they possess are in camels, kine, sheep, and goats, men servants and women servants, and changes of raiment; we may stand near one of their encampments, and as the aged men sit in dignity, or the young men and maidens drive past us their flocks, we are almost ready to ask if such a one be not Abraham, or Lot, or Jacob, or Job, or Bildad the Shuhite, or Rebekah, or Rachel, or the daughter of Jethro, the Midianite; we seem to know them all. The mountains, and valleys, and streams partake of the same unchangeableness; not a stone has been removed, not a barrier has been raised, not a tree has been planted, not a village has been collected together. The founder of the race might come again to the earth, and he would recognize, without effort, his own people and his own land." *

* Hardy's Tra els in the Holy Land, etc.

His hand will be against every man, and every man's hand against him.—Bearing in mind what has already been said respecting the *collective* import of the name Ishmael in this prediction,* we can have no difficulty in understanding this as a declaration that his posterity should exist in a state of perpetual hostility to the rest of mankind. And there is certainly no people to whom this applies with greater truth than to the Arabs; for there is none of whom aggression on all the world is so remarkably characteristic.† In the words of Gibbon, which strikingly correspond with those of the prophecy, "they are armed against mankind." They have all along infested Arabia and the neighbouring countries with their robberies and incursions. " Plunder, in fact, forms their principal occupation, and takes the chief place in their thoughts; and their aggressions upon settled districts, upon travellers, and even upon other tribes of their own people, are undertaken and prosecuted with a feeling that they have a right to what they seek, and therefore without the least sense of degradation. They have reduced robbery to a science, and digested its various branches into a complete and regular system."‡ " They regard the profession as honourable, and

* See page 43.   † Bush.   ‡ Pictorial Bible.

he character of a successful and enterprising
robber invests a Bedouin with as high a distinction in his own eyes, and in the eyes of his
people, as the most chivalrous acts would win
among the nations of Europe. The plundering
of a solitary traveller is in their eyes as much
a military exploit, as the sacking of a town, or
the reduction of a province."* " They rob in-
discriminately, enemies, friends, and neighbours. It is no protection to speak the same
language, or to profess the same religion. The
caravan on its pilgrimage to Mecca is considered to offer as lawful a booty as the bales of the
rich merchant, or the stores of the infidel
stranger."† Travellers crossing the desert are
compelled to go armed, in large companies or
caravans, and to keep watch and guard like a
little army, and then they scarcely ever escape
being plundered: even when they procure the
services of one of the Arabs as a guide, it only
ensures them protection from the assaults of
the tribe to which the guide belongs.

This plundering life they justify " by alleging the hard usage of their father Ishmael, who,
being turned out of doors by Abraham, had,
they say, the open plains and deserts given
him by God for his patrimony, with permission

* Chricton.   † Hardy.

to take whatever he could find there. And on this account they think they may, with a safe conscience, indemnify themselves as well as they can, not only on the descendants of Isaac, but on every body else; always supposing a sort of kindred between themselves and those they plunder. And in relating adventures of this kind, they think it sufficient to change the expression, and instead of saying, 'I robbed a man of such and such a thing,' to say, 'I gained it.'"[*]   But they do not confine their predatory excursions to the desert: they make frequent hostile inroads in the neighbouring countries, to supply those wants which the recesses of the desert have denied. "The poverty of their own land is with them an honourable excuse for relieving their necessities at the expense of their wealthier neighbours. They affirm that in the division of the earth, the rich and fertile parts were assigned to other branches of the human family; and that the descendants of the outlaw, whose hand was to be against every man, may recover, by force, the hereditary portion of which they have been unjustly deprived."[†]

This character of the Arabs, which is con-

[*] Sale's Preliminary Dissertation to the Koran.
[†] Chricton.

firmed by ancient history, and by every modern writer who has traversed their wide and barren wilds, is of itself sufficient to verify the prediction of the text. But besides this, the different tribes are continually at variance among themselves. Burckhardt assures us that there are few tribes which are ever in a state of perfect peace with all their neighbours, and adds, that he could not recollect this to be the case with any one among the numerous tribes with which he was acquainted. These wars, however, are seldom of long duration; peace is easily made, but broken again upon the slightest pretences.

This dark side of the Arab character has a beautiful contrast in their well known hospitality. The moment the fierce marauder ceases to be in a state of war, he becomes quite another man. The hungry Bedouin always divides his scanty meal with a still more hungry wanderer. The traveller who seeks his protection, or confides in his honour, he entertains without inquiry, or the hope of remuneration. He regards him not merely as a guest, but as a member of the family, and when he departs he is dismissed with blessings, perhaps with gifts. So long as he remains, his life and property are secure; and should a robbery occur, the host, if he possesses the means, will indemnify him for whatever loss he may incur while under his protection. The hospitality of the Arabs was greatly extolled in ancient times, and those of the present day exercise this virtue no less than their ancestors did.*

And he shall dwell in the presence of all his brethren.—The word translated "dwell," signifies literally to *tabernacle*, and refers to the practice of dwelling in tents, which has almost universally prevailed among the descendants of Ishmael, and to which there is an allusion in Isaiah xiii, 20. The meaning of the passage, taken in connection with the previous declaration, "He shall be a wild man," undoubtedly is, that the posterity of Ishmael, notwithstanding the constant hostility subsisting between them and other nations, should maintain a perpetual independence, and should continue to pitch their tents " in the presence," or in the face " of all their brethren," in spite of all attempts to conquer or dispossess them ; and nothing is more notorious than that they have never been effectually subdued ; although continually annoying the surrounding countries with their predatory incursions, yet every attempt to extirpate them has proved abortive, and they

* Chricton.—Niebuhr.

are at present, and have continued from the remotest ages, a separate, free, independent, and invincible nation.

The country in which they dwell lies between Egypt and Assyria, yet they were never subject to either of those powerful nations. Sesostris, the most renowned monarch that ever swayed the sceptre of Egypt, who, in the pride of his power, caused his chariot to be drawn by conquered kings, who were yoked to it like beasts of burden, was compelled, as Diodorus Siculus informs us, to draw a line of defence across the Isthmus of Suez, to secure his territory from the incessant depredations of the Arabs and Syrians. The Assyrians, Medes, and Persians found them alike invincible. Cambyses, when he invaded Egypt, was obliged to obtain permission of the Arabs to pass through their dominions ; and Cyrus, the deliverer of the Jews, and the conquerer of Babylon, could never impose conditions on this free, independent people. Herodotus, the historian who lived nearest those times, expressly states that " the Arabs were never reduced by the Persians to the condition of subjects, but were considered by them as friends, and opened to them a passage into Egypt, which without their assistance would have been utterly impracti-

cable." And in another place he says, that
"while Phenicia, Palestine, Syria, and all the
neighbouring countries were taxed, the Arabian
territory remained free from paying any tribute." Some time after we find them assisting the Egyptians against the Persians; so
that they appear to have acted as friends or
enemies to the Persians, as it suited their interests or inclinations.*

Alexander the Great, who overturned the
Persian empire, and conquered Asia, never
stretched his powerful sceptre over the wandering tribes of the desert. When other nations sent embassies of submission, the Arabs
alone disdained to acknowledge the conqueror,
and despised his menaces. Mortified at their
indifference, and determined to chastise their
presumption, he raised a prodigious force; but
death interposed; in the very midst of his purposes Alexander was cut off, and the Arabs
thus escaped the fury of his arms, and were
never subdued by any of his successors. We
find them afterward, sometimes at peace and
sometimes at war with the neighbouring states;
sometimes joining the Syrians, and sometimes
the Egyptians; sometimes assisting the Jews,
and sometimes plundering them; and in all

* Newton on the Prophecies.

respects acting like a free people who neither feared nor courted any foreign power whatever.*

In the course of time the sceptre of the world passed into the hands of the Romans : but while they subjected all other nations, they were never able to reduce Arabia to a Roman province, although at different periods of their power they made several attempts to do so. The flatterers of Trajan have, it is true, numbered among his exploits, the subjugation of all Arabia and part of India, and coins were actually struck in commemoration of these exploits ; but the most he was able to accomplish was the reduction of a few individual tribes ; the great body of the Arabs still continued with impunity to make incursions and depredations in Syria and the other Roman provinces, and eluded the vengeance of their enemies by retiring within those natural barriers of rocks and sand which bade defiance to their pursuers. " The Roman eagle, which spread her resistless pinions over all countries, and which neither the storms of the north could terrify, nor the supposed barriers of the world confine, found no- rest for the sole of its foot on the barren sands of Arabia, and returned unsuc-

* Newton.—Collyer.

cessful from the pursuit of the rough sons of Ishmael."

We have thus seen that the Arabs escaped the yoke of the most powerful nations of antiquity. Whoever were the conquerers of Asia, *they* remained free ; and they have transmitted their independence unimpaired to the present times. The descendants of the " wild man" still spurn the chains of a foreign conqueror. The Turks have now been for several centuries masters of the adjacent countries ; but their jurisdiction has never been acknowledged by the Arabs, and they are so little able to restrain the depredations of these fierce wanderers, that they are compelled to pay them a sort of tribute, in order to ensure the safe passage of the pilgrims who annually go in great companies or caravans to Mecca, and whom, after all, they frequently plunder with impunity.

But notwithstanding the united testimonies of ancient and modern history in favour of the uninterrupted freedom of the posterity of Ishmael, one writer has attempted to bring the alleged fulfilment of the prophecy into discredit. Mr. Gibbon, unwilling to pass by an opportunity of cavilling at divine revelation, observes, " The perpetual independence of the Arabs has been the theme of praise among

strangers and natives; and the arts of contro-
versy transform this singular event into a prophecy and a miracle, in favour of the posterity
of Ishmael. Some exceptions, that can neither
be dissembled nor eluded, render this mode of
reasoning as indiscreet as it is superfluous : the
kingdom of Yemen has been successfully subdued by the Abyssinians, the Persians, the sul-
tans of Egypt, and the Turks: the holy cities
of Mecca and Medina have repeatedly bowed
under a Scythian tyrant; and the Roman province of Arabia embraced the peculiar wilderness in which Ishmael and his sons must have
pitched their tent in the face of all their brethren." For a full reply to these unqualified
assertions, we need refer to no other writer
than Mr. Gibbon himself, who, by the conces-
sion which he is compelled to make upon the
truth of an historian, furnishes a complete re-
futation to his own objections. In the passage immediately following the one we have
just quoted, without the intervention of a single
sentence, he says, " Yet these exceptions are
temporary or *local;* the body of the nation has
escaped the yoke of the most powerful mo-
narchies ; the arms of Sesostris and Cyrus, of
Pompey and Trajan, *could never achieve the conquest of Arabia;* the present sovereign of the

Turks may exercise a shadow of jurisdiction, but his pride is reduced to solicit the friendship of *a people whom it is dangerous to provoke,* and *fruitless to attack.* The long memory of their independence is the firmest pledge of its perpetuity; and succeeding generations are animated to prove their descent, and to maintain their inheritance. Their domestic feuds are suspended on the approach of a common enemy; and in their last hostilities against the Turks, the caravan of Mecca was attacked and pillaged by fourscore thousand of the confederates. When they advance to battle, the hope of victory is in their front, and in the rear the assurance of a retreat. Their horses and camels, who in eight or ten days can perform a journey of four or five hundred miles, disappear before the conqueror; the secret waters of the desert elude his search, and his victorious troops are consumed with thirst, hunger, and fatigue, in the pursuit of an invisible foe, who scorns his efforts, and safely reposes in the heart of the burning solitude." Yemen is the only Arabian province which had the appearance of submitting to a foreign yoke; but even here, as Mr. Gibbon himself acknowledges, seven of the native princes remained unsubdued; and even admitting its subjugation to have been complete, the perpetual independence of the Ishmaelites remains unimpaired, *for this is not their country*.

The accounts given of the Arabs by travellers fully accord with the prophecy respecting them. Sandys remarks, " They dwell in tents, which they remoue, like walking cities, for opportunity of prey, and benefit of pasturage. They acknowledge no soueraigne: not worth the conquering, nor can they bee conquered: retiring to places impassable for armies, by reason of the rolling sands, and penury of all things. A nation from the beginning vnmixed with others: boasting of their nobilitie, and at this day hating all mechanicall sciences. They hang about the skirts of the habitable countries; and hauing robbed, retire with a maruellous celerity."

Volney, in his account of the Bedouins, observes, " It is not without reason that the inhabitants of the desert boast of being the purest and best preserved race of all the Arab tribes: for *never have they been conquered*, nor have they mixed with other people by making conquests; they have in every respect retained their primitive independence and simplicity. Every thing that ancient history has related of their cus-

toms, manners, language, and even their prejudices, is almost minutely true of them to this
day ; and if we consider, besides, this unity of
character, preserved through such a number of
ages, still subsists, even in the most distant
situations, that is, that the tribes most distant
from each other preserve an exact resemblance,
it must be allowed, that the circumstances
which accompany so peculiar a moral state are
a subject of most curious inquiry."

How is it that this remarkable people have
never changed their situation, or altered their
habits of life ? Other nations have not continued the same. How have the modern population of Egypt, Italy, and Greece, degenerated
from the powerful nations who formerly occupied those countries ? How are the French
and English polished and refined from the ancient Gauls and Britons ? Men and manners
change with times, but in all ages the Arabs
have continued essentially the same. The
character of Ishmael remains unobliterated in
the features of his descendants, and, at the close
of thirty-seven centuries, they still continue, in
accordance with the prophetic description, a
numerous people, living in a state of wild and
lawless independence.

Who can fairly consider all these particulars, and not see the hand of God in the whole affair, from the beginning to the end. It was impossible for any human eye to have pierced the cloud of unveiled time; or for any uninspired tongue to have foretold the destinies of this outcast child, and of his unborn descendants. But He who collects into one point of view the past, the present, and the future, as scattered rays of light are sometimes collected in a common centre, uttered the memorable prediction, whose fulfilment we have just been considering—a prediction, the fulfilment of which was, in the natural course of events, so highly improbable, if not altogether impossible, that, as nothing but a divine prescience could have foreseen it, so nothing but a divine power could have brought it to pass. "Of no other, among all the streams of population by which this earth has been covered, was such a prophecy uttered; and of no other would it have been true. The surrounding countries of Egypt, Syria, and Persia, have once and again changed their rulers and their race. Arabia has ever continued the same. The march of conquest has been around her, but has never penetrated into her wilds: that which was true of her in the time of Moses, has been equally so in every subsequent period of time ; and will still continue until another prophecy be fulfilled, and even ' Arabia's desert ranger' shall bow before the power that is supreme : then the horse shall no longer stand ready caparisoned to pursue and plunder the passing traveller ; ' Holiness unto the Lord,' shall be inscribed ' upon its bells ;' then shall Isaac and Ishmael again meet together in peace, to worship at one altar the God of their fathers, and Jesus Christ whom he has sent : their hand shall be *with* every man, and every man's hand with them."*

* Hardy.

CHAPTER III.

PROPHECIES CONCERNING THE JEWS.

The purpose of God in raising up the Jewish nation—Their covenant with God at Sinai—Their covenant solemnly renewed on mounts Ebal and Gerizim—Calamities which awaited them if they violated the commands of God—Blessings promised in case of obedience—Moses foresaw and foretold their future apostacy, and the evils which would consequently befall them—They were to be invaded by a distant nation, who should treat them with extreme cruelty, and take from them all their cities—This prophecy fully accomplished by the Romans—The miseries which, from famine and other causes, they endured in the course of the war—Great numbers sold as slaves, and sent into Egypt—The sanctuaries are brought into desolation—The great body of the people are driven out of their own land—The few who remain there are miserably oppressed—The Jews are dispersed among all nations.

No prophecies better deserve the attention of the Biblical student, or more clearly establish the truth of divine revelation, than those respecting the Jews, a people raised up by Providence, in a time of general apostacy, to preserve, through the darkness of succeeding ages, the light of the knowledge of God.

The waters of the deluge had scarce dried up from the face of the earth, when the sons of men again began to work iniquity in the sight of their Maker; and the venerable patriarch " who had seen the whole human race, his own family excepted, cut off for their wickedness,

lived to see the descendants of that family become almost as numerous and as profligate as
the generation which had been destroyed by
the flood." That the knowledge of the one
true God might not be utterly banished from
the earth, the Lord determined to set apart one
people to be the witnesses of his grace and the
depositaries of his truth, that he might thus
" preserve his testimony among the nations until
the arrival of that ' time of refreshing' which
he had predetermined, and the coming of which
he made known with increasing distinctness,
as its date approached. To accomplish this
object, Jehovah did not see fit to make choice
of any existing nation, but determined to give
a nation existence, to watch over it from its
birth, subjecting its infancy to his guidance and
instruction, and forming its character with a
view to the great object of its being."*

The early history of the Jewish nation is one
unbroken series of divine interpositions. At
the age of seventy-five years, Abraham journeyed from the land of the Chaldeans, not knowing whither he went, " but obeying a divine
voice which called him from among a nation of
idolaters, to become the father of a new people, and of a purer faith, at a distance from his

* Pictorial History of Palestine.

native country." Led by the Spirit of God, he entered the land of Canaan, where Jehovah appeared to him, promised that he would multiply his posterity as the stars of heaven, and as the sand upon the sea-shore, and give them that land for an inheritance; and assured him that in his "seed should all the families of the earth be blessed," Gen. xii, 7; xxii, 17, 18. Two hundred and fifteen years after this, his grandson Jacob, "a Syrian ready to perish," with a few individuals, went down into Egypt, where his descendants, although "evil entreated and afflicted," "became a nation great, mighty, and populous," (Deut. xxvi, 5,) and whence they were delivered by the special interposition of Heaven. Guided by "a pillar of cloud by day, and a pillar of fire by night," they proceeded to Mount Sinai, where they entered into a solemn covenant with God, to serve and obey him. Under circumstances of the most terrific grandeur, Jehovah then delivered to the people the moral law, or the ten commandments; after which, he communicated to Moses the laws by which they were to be governed as a nation, and the ceremonies to be observed in their religious worship. Forty years they were condemned to wander in the wilderness as a punishment for their sins, during which, time the

Lord fed them with "bread from heaven," and
"gave them water out of the flinty rock."

When at length they approached the borders
of the land of Canaan, and viewed, for the first
time, their promised inheritance, Moses, then
about to surrender at once both his life and his
trust, recounted, in the ears of the people, the
mercies of God toward them, and the many de-
liverances he had wrought out for them. He
then assured them that their prosperity in the
land which they were now about to enter, de-
pended entirely upon their conformity to the
divine precepts, and urged upon them the duty
and necessity of obedience, as well from a consideration of the goodness of God and the blessings that should follow, as from the fearful
judgments which awaited them in case of their
apostacy.

That these admonitions might make a more
lasting impression on the minds of the people,
Moses directed Joshua that as soon as they entered the promised land, he should lead them
to mounts Ebal and Gerizim, and there solemnly renew their covenant with God. Six of the
tribes were to stand on the side of mount Gerizim, and the remaining six on mount Ebal, opposite, while the priests and the Levites, with
the ark of the covenant, occupied the narrow

valley between: when the priests read from the book of the law the blessings which should be the reward of their obedience, the tribes on mount Gerizim responded, " Amen !" *So be it !* while the tribes on the opposite mountain gave a like response to the curses which were denounced on the disobedient. Deut. xxvii, xxviii.

It is impossible for human imagination to conceive a spectacle more imposing, more solemn, more likely to impress the whole people with deep and enduring awe, than this final ratification of their covenant, as directed by the dying lawgiver.   In the open day, and in a theatre, as it were, created by the God of nature for the express purpose,* after a sacrifice offered on an altar of stones, the people of Israel testified their deliberate acceptance of that constitution which God had enacted for them.   They accepted it with its inseparable conditions, maledictions

* "A better situation for performing his ceremony," observes Mr. Hardy, "could not be conceived; as the hills are at such a distance from each other, that the hosts of Israel might stand between their summits, and the voice from either be heard distinctly, on a calm day, throughout the whole assembly." The two mountains are each about seven hundred feet in height, and are separated only by the narrow valley of Shechem, which is not more than two or three hundred paces broad.

the most awful, which they imprecated on their own heads, in case they should violate its statutes—blessings equally ample and perpetual, if they should adhere to its holy and salutary provisions.* When the countless multitudes which thronged the ascent of either mountain, with one voice responded the loud "Amen!" as the blessings and curses were severally pronounced by the priests, the full burst of sound " must have reverberated among the hills with true sublimity, and have ascended in majestic volume toward heaven."

Having given the necessary directions for the performance of this impressive ceremony, Moses proceeded to enlarge on the blessings of obedience; but, with a dark and melancholy foreboding of the final destiny of his people, he laid before them, still more at length, the fatal consequences of apostacy and wickedness. The sublimity of his denunciations surpasses any thing in the oratory or the poetry of the whole world. Nature is exhausted in furnishing terrific images; nothing excepting the real horrors of the Jewish history—the miseries of their sieges, the cruelty, the contempt, the oppressions, the persecutions, which for ages this scattered, and despised, and detested nation has

* Rev. H. H. Millman.

endured—can approach the tremendous maledictions which warned them against the violation of their law.*   These prophetic denunciations are contained in the twenty-eighth chapter
of Deuteronomy, from which we give the following extracts :—

"It shall come to pass, if thou wilt not hearken
unto the voice of the Lord thy God, to observe
to do all his commandments,—the Lord shall
cause thee to be smitten before thy enemies :
thou shalt go out one way against them, and flee
seven ways before them : and shalt be removed
into all the kingdoms of the earth.—The Lord
shall smite thee with madness, and blindness, and
astonishment of heart : and thou shalt grope at
noonday, as the blind gropeth in darkness, and
thou shalt not prosper in thy ways : and thou shalt
be only oppressed and spoiled evermore, and no
man shall save thee.—Thine ox shall be slain
before thine eyes, and thou shalt not eat thereof :
thine ass shall be violently taken away from
before thy face, and shall not be restored to
thee ; thy sheep shall be given to thine enemies, and thou shalt have none to rescue them.
Thy sons and thy daughters shall be given unto
another people, and thine eyes shall look, and

* Rev. H H. Millman.

fail with longing for them all the day long.—
The fruit of thy land, and all thy labour, shall
a nation which thou knowest not eat up ; and
thou shalt be only oppressed and crushed always : so that thou shalt be mad for the sight
of thine eyes which thou shalt see.—The Lord
shall bring thee, and thy king which thou shalt
set over thee, unto a nation which neither thou
nor thy fathers have known ; and there shalt
thou serve other gods, wood and stone.   And
thou shalt become an astonishment, a proverb,
and a by-word among all nations whither the
Lord shall lead thee.—The stranger that is within thee shall get up above thee very high ; and
thou shalt come down very low. He shall lend to
thee, and thou shalt not lend to him : he shall be
the head, and thou shalt be the tail.*   All these
curses shall come upon thee because thou heark-
enest not unto the voice of the Lord thy God,
to keep his commandments ; and they shall be

* The "head" and the "tail" are common forms of expression in the East, to denote the most elevated and the
most degraded conditions.   Mr. Roberts, in his Oriental
Illustrations, observes, "It is amusing to hear men of rank
in the East speak of their dependants as *tails*.   Has a servant not obeyed his master, the former asks, 'Who are
you? are you the head or the tail?'   Should a person begin to take food before those of higher caste, it is asked,
'What, is the tail to begin to wag before the head?'"

upon thee for a sign and for a wonder, and upon thy seed for ever. The Lord shall bring a nation against thee from far, from the end of the earth, as swift as the eagle flieth; a nation whose tongue thou shalt not understand; a nation of fierce countenance, which shall not regard the person of the old, nor show favour to the young.—And he shall besiege thee in all thy gates, until thy high and fenced walls come down, wherein thou trustedst, throughout all thy land, which the Lord thy God hath given thee. And thou shalt eat the fruit of thine own body, the flesh of thy sons and of thy daughters, in the siege, and in the straitness wherewith thine enemies shall distress thee; the man that is tender among you, and very delicate, his eye shall be evil toward his brother, and toward the wife of his bosom, and toward the remnant of his children which he shall leave: so that he will not give to any of them the flesh of his children which he shall eat: because he hath nothing left him of the siege, and in the straitness wherewith thine enemies shall distress thee in all thy gates. The tender and delicate woman among you, which would not adventure to set the sole of her foot upon the ground for delicateness and tenderness, her eye shall be evil toward the husband of her bosom, and toward her son, and toward her daughter, and toward her children which she shall bear : for she shall eat them for the want of all things, secretly in the siege and straitness wherewith thine enemies shall distress thee.—The Lord will make thy plagues wonderful, and the plagues of thy seed, even great plagues, and of long continuance.—And ye shall be left few in number, whereas ye were as the stars of heaven for multitude; because thou wouldst not obey the voice of the Lord thy God.—And ye shall be plucked from off the land whither thou goest to possess it. And the Lord shall scatter thee among all people, from one end of the earth even unto the other. —And among these nations shalt thou find no ease, neither shall the sole of thy foot have rest : but the Lord shall give thee there a trembling heart,—and thy life shall hang in doubt before thee ; and thou shalt have fear day and night, and shalt have none assurance of thy life. In the morning thou shalt say, ' Would God it were even!' and at even thou shalt say, ' Would God it were morning!' for the fear of thine heart wherewith thou shalt fear, and for the sight of thine eyes which thou shalt see. And the Lord shall bring thee again into Egypt with ships,—and there ye shall be sold unto your enemies for bondmen and bondwomen, and no man shall buy you."

Such were the judgments with which Moses, by the authority of God, threatened the Israelites in case of their disobedience. On the other hand, corresponding blessings were promised if they remained faithful to God, and kept their covenant with him. "It shall come to pass if thou wilt hearken diligently to the voice of the Lord thy God, to observe to do all his commandments, that the Lord thy God will set thee on high above all the nations of the earth.—The Lord shall cause thine enemies that rise up against thee to be smitten before thy face.—The Lord shall make thee plenteous in goods, —and in the fruit of thy ground;—and he shall bless thee in the land which the Lord thy God giveth thee. The Lord shall establish thee a holy people unto himself,—and all the people of the earth shall see that thou art called by the name of the Lord, and they shall be afraid of thee."

Thus the national prosperity of the Israelites was made to depend on their obedience to God. No attentive reader of the Bible can have failed to perceive how strikingly this was the case through the whole period of their Scripture history. "If they yield to disobedience or

idolatry, the meanest of their neighbours, Moabites, Midianites, Amalekites, even the subject
and tributary Canaanites, can rise in arms to
their discomfiture and degradation.   Let them
serve the Lord faithfully, and 'one' of them
may 'chase a thousand,' the 'daughter of Zion'
may 'shake her head' at the countless hosts of
the 'great king, the king of Assyria.' "*

The denunciations of Moses are to be regarded not merely as conditional threatenings,
but as clear and distinct predictions.   Instructed by the spirit of prophecy, he not only warned the people of the consequences of disobedience, but also foresaw and plainly foretold
their future apostacy; " I know," said he, " that
after my death ye will utterly corrupt your-
selves, and turn aside from the way which I
have commanded you; and evil will befall you
in the latter days; because ye will do evil in
the sight of the Lord, to provoke him to anger
with the work of your hands," Deut. xxxi, 29.
See also verses 16–21.

To notice all the prophecies of Scripture respecting the Jews, would occupy a volume,
and embrace the whole history of that people
from their first existence to the present time;

* Professor Fausett.

we shall, therefore, give our attention chiefly to some of the most striking prophecies of Moses, which, although partially fulfilled in every apostacy and calamity of the Jews, and especially in their subjection by Nebuchadnezzar, yet refer more directly to their final and fearful overthrow by the Romans, and their subsequent dispersion over the face of the whole earth. In our notices of these predictions, we shall take them up as nearly as possible in the order of their fulfilment.

" *The Lord shall bring a nation against thee from far, from the end of the earth, as swift as the eagle flieth, a nation whose tongue thou shalt not understand.*"—A description very similar to this is given of the Chaldeans by Jeremiah:— " Lo, I will bring a nation upon you from far, O house of Israel, saith the Lord:—a nation whose language thou knowest not, neither understandest what they say," Jer. v, 15. He also compares them to eagles :—" Our persecutors are swifter than the eagles of heaven," Lam. iv, 19. But the description of Moses, in its full extent, can be applied to none of the invaders of Judea with so much propriety as to the Romans. They truly came " from far, from the ends of the earth." The soldiers composing the armies with which they subdued Palestine were mostly from Gaul,* Spain, and Britain, countries which formed the limits of the then known world. The Roman generals, Vespasian and Adrian, who were the two greatest instruments in the destruction of the Jews, both came for that purpose from Britain, which in those days was considered and denominated the *end of the earth.* Indeed, it is said that the soldiers of Cesar were unwilling to follow him to the conquest of Britain, because they imagined that he was passing the limits of the world. The " eagle" was the standard of the Roman armies, and the flight of that bird was an apt and forcible representation of the rapidity of their conquests. The language of the Romans, too, was far more unintelligible to the Jews than was that of the Chaldeans : Dr. A. Clarke says that the Latin tongue is more foreign than any other to the structure and idiom of the Hebrew.

The invaders of Judea are further characterized as " *a nation of fierce countenance,*† *which*

* The ancient name of France.

† This expression will remind the historical reader of the language of Pyrrhus, king of Epirus, who, after an engagement in which he obtained a victory over the Ro-

shall not regard the person of the old, nor show favour to the young."—This was true of both the Chaldeans and the Romans in their treatment of the conquered Jews. Of the former it is said that they " slew their young men with the sword,—and had no compassion upon young man or maiden, old man or him that stooped with age," 2 Chron. xxxvi, 17. The Romans were of a haughty, warlike spirit, but the history of their conduct toward other nations furnishes no parallel to the inflexible, unrelenting, indiscriminate cruelty which they exercised toward the Jews. When they took Gadara, " they slew all the youth, having no mercy on any age whatever."* On the capture of Japha, " after the fighting men were killed, they cut the throats of the rest of the multitude, partly in the open air, partly in their own houses, both young and old ; so that there were no males remaining except infants, who, with the women, were carried as slaves into captivity."† The whole number killed in the fight and the sub-

mans, was walking about the field of battle ; and seeing the wounds of the Romans all in front, and marking the fierceness of their countenance, preserved even in death, he exclaimed, that if he had such soldiers he would subdue the world.—*Collyer's Lectures.*

* Josephus, Wars, book iii, chap. 7. † Ibid.

sequent slaughter amounted to fifteen thousand.

The inhabitants of Jotapata, to the number
of forty thousand, met with a similar fate.* On
taking Tarichea, Vespasian gave the inhabitants an assurance that their lives should be
spared, but compelled them to leave the place,
and go to Tiberias, where, in violation of his
promise, he barbarously slew all the " old men,
together with others that were useless, who
were in number twelve hundred." Of the remainder, upward of thirty thousand were sold
as slaves.† When they took Gamala, they
slew all the inhabitants they found in it, without regard to age or sex; they spared not so
much as the infants, of whom many were flung
down by them from the citadel. None escaped
except two women who hid themselves.‡

> " Patient submission and resistance met
>   One common fate : the snowy locks of age
>   In dust and gore lay clotted : nor the blush
>   That mantled on the lovely virgin's cheek,
>   Alternate yielding to the paly hue
>   Of blanching fear ; nor the mute eloquence
>   Of helpless infancy, that playful smiled
>   In its destroyer's face, could mercy find."

The Jews in Palestine were not the only suf-

---

* Josephus, Wars, book iii, chap. 7.   † Ibid.
‡ Ibid., book iv, chap. 1.

ferers in this war.   At Alexandria, in Egypt, a conflict arose between the Jews and the other inhabitants of that city, in consequence of which the Roman governor sent two legions of soldiers and five thousand other troops to attack the quarter of the city in which the Jews resided, with orders to slay the people and set fire to their houses.   "The soldiers did as they were bidden;—no mercy was shown to the infants, and no regard had to the aged; but they went on in the slaughter of persons of every age, till all the place was overflowed with blood, and fifty thousand of them lay dead upon heaps."*

"*And he shall besiege thee in all thy gates, until thy high and fenced walls come down, wherein thou trustedst, in all thy land.*"—The cities of the Jews were mostly built in commanding positions, and strongly defended by art.   This was especially the case with Samaria and Jerusalem, which, in the ancient mode of warfare, were considered almost impregnable.   But strong natural positions and massive fortifications could not protect an ungodly people from the threatened judgments of the Almighty. When Israel forsook the Lord, her defence departed from her, and her strong cities fell into

* Josephus, Wars, book ii, chap. 18.

the hands of her enemies. "In the reign of Ho-
shea, king of Israel, Shalmaneser, king of Assyria, came up against Samaria, and besieged it;
and at the end of three years they took it: and the
king of Assyria did carry away all Israel unto
Assyria;—because they obeyed not the voice
of the Lord their God, but transgressed his covenant, and all that Moses, the servant of the
Lord, commanded," 2 Chron. xviii, 9–12.   In
the reign of Zedekiah, king of Judah, Jerusalem, after a siege of two years, was taken
by Nebuchadnezzar, who brake down its walls,
and carried the people of Judah into captivity.
And finally, when the Jews had filled the measure of their iniquity, by rejecting and crucify-
ing the Saviour, the Romans under Titus, and
afterward under Adrian, " came and took away
their place and nation." Every fortress was
reduced, every city was taken, the walls of Jerusalem were broken down, and the city utterly
destroyed; and since that period the Jews have
never possessed a town or a strong hold in
their native land.

The prophecy then goes on to show the extremities of famine to which, in the course of
these sieges, the people would be reduced.
" And thou shalt eat the fruit of thine own body,

the flesh of thy sons and of thy daughters, in the siege, and in the straitness wherewith thine enemies shall distress thee."—This terrible denunciation has been more than once fulfilled. Six hundred years after the time of Moses, Samaria, the metropolis of the kingdom of Israel, endured the first of those dreadful sieges by which the two capitals of the Jewish kingdoms appear, by some awful fatality, to have been distinguished beyond all the other cities of the world. So great was the famine in the city on this occasion, that the most worthless substitutes for food were sold at an enormous price, and a woman " boiled her son and did eat him," 2 Kings vi, 24–29. Jeremiah pathetically describes the horrors of the famine in Jerusalem when it was besieged by Nebuchadnezzar, and closes his description by saying, " The hands of pitiful women have sodden their own children ; they were their meat in the destruction of the daughter of my people," Lam. iv, 3–10. But the unparalleled sufferings of the Jews by famine during the siege of Jerusalem by Titus, far exceed any thing of the kind which they, or any other people, ever before endured. The account is given by Josephus, who was himself present at the siege. He says,—" The famine overcame all other passions ;" filial re-

verence and parental affection were alike forgotten; "children snatched from the mouths
of their fathers the very food they were eating;
and what was still more to be pitied, the mothers did the same as to their infants: and
when those that were most dear were perishing under their hands, they were not ashamed
to take from them the very last drops that might
preserve their lives."* "If so much as the
shadow of any kind of food did anywhere appear, a war was presently commenced, and the
dearest friends fell to fighting one with another
about it, snatching from each other the most
miserable supports of life."† "Famine devoured the people by whole houses and families:
the upper rooms were full of women and children that were dying of hunger, and the lanes
of the city were full of the dead bodies of the
aged; the children and the young men wandered about the market-places like shadows, all
swelled with the famine, and fell down dead
wheresoever their misery seized them."‡—
"Some persons were driven to such terrible
distress as to search the common sewers and
old dung-hills of cattle, and what they before
could not endure so much as to see, they now

* Wars, book v, chap. 10.   † Ibid., book vi, chap. 3.
‡ Ibid., book v, chap. 12.

used for food."* Little do those who are surrounded by plenty know what are the horrors of famine, and to what extremities human nature may be driven. But the most horrible incident yet remains to be told; an incident in itself so incredible that Josephus declares he would not have related it, had there not been at the time he wrote innumerable living witnesses of its truth. A lady of high consideration, "eminent for her family and her wealth," had been plundered of all her substance and provisions by the soldiers, who endeavoured to sustain themselves during the famine by breaking into private houses, and robbing the occupants of what little food they had. Driven to madness and desperation by her hunger, she killed the child that was sucking at her breast, "and then roasted him, ate one half of him, and secreted the remainder." Allured by the smell of dressed meat, the soldiers rushed into the house, and threatened to kill her if she did not show them what food she had gotten. With bitter irony she assured them that a fine portion had been saved for them, and then produced the half-eaten body of her child; when they were struck with horror and amazement at the sight, she said to them, "This

* Wars, book v, chap. 13.

is mine own son, and what hath been done was mine own doing. Come, eat of this food, for I have eaten of it myself. Do not pretend to be either more tender than a woman, or more compassionate than a mother. But if you be so scrupulous, and do abominate this my sacrifice, as I have eaten the one half, let the rest be left for me also." Upon this the men went out trembling and affrighted; and the story being soon spread over the city, did so affect the famishing people, that they desired nothing so much as to die, and esteemed those already dead to be happy, since they had not lived long enough either to hear or to see such miseries.* How strikingly did these events fulfil the prophecies of Moses, uttered at least fifteen hundred years before! " The tender and delicate woman among you, which would not adventure to set the sole of her foot upon the ground for delicateness and tenderness, her eye shall be evil toward the husband of her bosom, and toward her son, and toward her daughter,—*and toward her children which she shall bear, for she shall eat them for the want of all things secretly* in the siege and straitness wherewith thine enemy shall distress thee in thy gates." Deut. xxviii, 56, 57.

* Josephus, Wars, book vi, chapter 2.

It was also foretold that their numbers would be greatly diminished by the calamities that should overtake them. *" Ye shall be left few in number, whereas ye were as the stars of heaven for multitude."*—This prediction was fearfully accomplished in the immense slaughters of the Jews which took place during their contests with the Romans. From the accounts furnished by Josephus, the number of Jews who were destroyed in the course of the war which terminated in the capture of Jerusalem by Titus, must have been little less than a million and a half; eleven hundred thousand perished in the siege of Jerusalem alone. About forty-five years after the close of this war, the Jews in Egypt and Cyprus revolted, and slew upward of four hundred thousand of the inhabitants of those countries; but although they obtained at first some partial successes, yet they were finally defeated by the Romans under Adrian, who afterward became emperor of Rome. The murders committed by the Jews in the commencement of the insurrection were fearfully retaliated by the conquerors. The loss of the Jews was immense: according to their own traditions, as many fell in this disastrous war as originally escaped from Egypt under Moses—six hundred thousand men. About fifteen years after this, the standard of revolt was again raised by an individual who assumed the name of Barchobab, *The son of a star*, and pretended to be the Messiah. The Jews at once hailed him as their promised deliverer, and the insurrection soon spread through the whole of Palestine. The insurgents obtained possession of the ruined site of Jerusalem, and made themselves masters of most of the strong holds in the country; but after a contest of nearly five years, they were entirely subdued by the Romans under Adrian and Severus. The historian Dio Cassins states, that during this war five hundred and eighty thousand Jews were slain, besides those who perished by famine, disease, and fire. In consequence of these desolating wars, the people who had been " as the stars of heaven for multitude," were " left few in number;" the land of Judea was almost deserted, and wild beasts went howling along the streets of the desolate cities.

Besides the immense multitudes thus destroyed, vast numbers were reduced to slavery. Of the captives taken by Titus at the siege of Jerusalem " those above seventeen years of age were sent bound to Egypt to work in the mines;" those under that age were sold, and " at a very low price, because the numbers sold were so great, and the purchasers but few." Indeed, so little value was set upon the captives, that " eleven thousand of them were suffered to perish for want of food." " The whole number of those who were carried captive during this war, amounted to ninety-seven thousand."* " After their last overthrow by Adrian, many thousands of them were sold; and those who could not be sold were transported into Egypt, and perished by shipwreck, or famine, or were massacred by the inhabitants."† Fifteen hundred years before this, when the Israelites had just been triumphantly delivered from the bondage of Egypt, Moses specified among the judgments that should befall them, that they should again be carried into Egypt as slaves, and in such numbers that purchasers should not be found for them:—" *And the Lord shall bring thee into Egypt again with ships; and there ye shall be sold unto your enemies for bondmen and for bondwomen, and no man shall buy you.*" " Egypt, indeed, was the great slave mart of ancient times, and several of the conquerors of the Jews had before sent, at least, a large proportion of their captives thither to be sold."‡

* Josephus, Wars, book vi, chapters 8 and 9.
† St. Jerome, as quoted by Bishop Newton.
‡ Pictorial Bible.

"*I will bring your sanctuaries into desolation,*" Lev. xxvi, 31.—The word "sanctuaries," is here used to denote those places which were set apart for the service and worship of God, especially the temple. These were destroyed when Jerusalem was taken by the Chaldeans. From 2 Kings xxv, 8, 9, we learn that they "burned the house of the Lord;" and in Psalm lxiv, 7, 8, it is said,—

> "They have cast fire into thy sanctuary,
> They have defiled by casting down the dwelling-place
>   of thy name to the ground.
> They said in their hearts, 'Let us destroy them together:'
> They have burned up all the synagogues of God in the
>   land."

On the return of the Jews from the Babylonish captivity, the temple was rebuilt, and was standing when Jerusalem was besieged by the Romans. When the city was taken, the Roman commander was greatly desirous to preserve this building from the general destruction;

> "But Cesar could not save what God had doom'd,"

and, in spite of his utmost efforts, the second temple shared the fate of its predecessor.

"*And ye shall be plucked from off the land whither thou goest to possess it.*"—This prediction was accomplished, first, when Shalmanezer "carried Israel away into Assyria," (2 Kings xvii, 6,) again, when Nebuchadnezzar carried Judah captive to Babylon, and, finally, when the great body of the Jews were driven out of their country by the Romans under Titus and Adrian. That he might effectually destroy any hopes the Jews might still entertain of re-establishing themselves in Palestine, Adrian founded a new city on the site of Jerusalem, and peopled it with foreigners. He also placed the image of a swine over one of the gates; and, on pain of death, prohibited any Jew from entering the city, or even approaching so near as to view from a distance its sacred height. "Tertullian and Jerome say, they were prohibited from entering Judea."* It is certain that since that period comparatively few Jews have been found there. "While the country has been successfully overrun by Greeks, Christians, Saracens, and Turks, the ancient poprietors of the soil have alone been denied a possession therein."† Sandys, who visited Palestine in 1611, says, the country "is for the most part now inhabited by Moores and Arabians;—Turkes there be few, but many Greekes, with other Christians of all sects and nations. Here be also some Iewes, yet inherit they no

* Bishop Newton.   † Pictorial Bible.

7

part of the land, but in their owne country do live as aliens." The number of Jews now living in Palestine is probably not more than twelve thousand, of whom about one half are to be found in Jerusalem, and the remainder principally at Hebron, Tiberias, and Saphet, these four places being regarded by them with peculiar and superstitious veneration.

That, after their expulsion, a miserable remnant would continue to be found in the land of their fathers, was intimated by the prophet, who in the following words clearly foretold the abject condition to which they should be reduced, and the haughty deportment of their rulers toward them:—"*The stranger that is within thee shall get up above thee very high, and thou shalt come down very low.*"—The condition of the Jews in Palestine has for many centuries furnished a striking commentary on this prediction. "They have not only lived as aliens in the land that was once their own, but of all the aliens found in that land, *they* are the most oppressed and degraded."* "Their condition is more insecure, and exposed to insult and oppression, than in Egypt and Syria, from the frequent lawless and oppressive conduct of the governors and chiefs."† Van Egmont and Hey

* Pictorial Bible.   † Carne's Letters from the East.

nam, speaking of the Jews at Saphet, observes : —" The Turks, by a variety of oppressions, fines, and the like unjust practices, squeeze them to such a degree that they may be said to pay for the very air they breathe. They lead the poorest and most deplorable life that can be conceived." The author of " Three Weeks in Palestine" thus describes their condition in Jerusalem :—" Every thing about them exhibited signs of depression and misery : they are outcasts from the common rights and sympathies of man ; oppressed and despised alike by Mohammedans and Christians." They are said to consist chiefly of persons advanced in life, who come to Palestine from various parts of the earth, and submit to these oppressions, that they may have the satisfaction of spending their remaining days in the land of Israel, and lay their bones in the sepulchres of their fathers.

They were not only to be thrust out of their own land, but also to be dispersed through the whole world. *" The Lord shall scatter thee among all people, from one end of the earth even unto the other."*—And where on the face of the earth is there a trading nation in which the Jews are unknown ? They have been spread over every province of the habitable globe ; they have used almost every tongue, have lived in every climate, and under every form of government. " Neither mountains, nor rivers, nor deserts, nor oceans,—which are the boundaries of other nations,—have terminated their wanderings." They abound in Turkey, Poland, Holland, Russia, Prussia, Austria, Germany, and the northern states of Africa, especially Tunis and Morocco. In Italy, Portugal, France, Britain, Hindostan, Persia, Egypt, and the United States, they are more thinly scattered. They have long been established in China, which abhors the foreigner, and in Abyssinia, which it is almost as difficult to reach as to quit. They are found also in New-Holland, Japan, and the West Indies; in Switzerland, Sweden, and the isles of Greece; on the rock of Gibraltar, and at the Cape of Good Hope. They have drunk of the Tiber, the Thames, and the Tigris; of the Niger, the Ganges, and the Mississippi. " They have trodden the snows of Siberia, and the sands of the burning desert; and the European traveller hears of their existence in regions which he cannot reach,—even in the very interior of Africa, south of Timbuctoo." In a word, they are to be found everywhere, and are everywhere living witnesses of the divine foresight, government, and veracity.

CHAPTER IV.

THE PROPHECIES CONCERNING THE JEWS: CONCLUDED.

The Jews, according to the prophecy, are everywhere persecuted and oppressed—Their treatment by Mohammed and his followers—Their treatment in Christian countries, Spain, Germany, France, England—Striking accordance between the language of prophecy and the facts of history—The Jews are violently deprived of their children—They become a proverb and by-word among all people—Were often driven to desperation by their calamities—The greatness and duration of their plagues—Their wonderful preservation in spite of every effort to destroy them—While the Jews have been preserved, the great nations who formerly oppressed them are utterly extinct—The Jews a standing miracle and a perpetual evidence of the truth of the Bible—Promises of their conversion—Probable causes why so few have as yet been converted—Increase of interest on the subject of their conversion—Extracts from the report of a deputation sent by the Church of Scotland to visit the Jews in various parts of the world, and ascertain the prospects of a mission among them—The Jews have greater claims upon Christians than have any other people—Extract from St. Paul—Hymn by Charles Wesley.

IT is our purpose in this chapter to follow the Jews in their dispersion, and exhibit the fulfilment of the prophecies which relate to the treatment they should meet with in the various countries whither they were driven.

"*And among these nations shalt thou have no ease, neither shall the sole of thy foot have rest, but the Lord shall give thee a trembling heart, and failing of eyes, and sorrow of mind:—and*

thou shalt be only oppressed and spoiled evermore."
—How remarkably have these predictions been
accomplished in the entire history of the Jews
since their final dispersion! The terrible
calamities which befell them in their contests
with the power of Rome were but " the beginning of sorrows." Their expulsion from Judea
was only the prelude to the various banish-
ments, persecutions, and oppressions which in
every age, and in almost every part of the world,
have been the lot of this unhappy race. Tertullian, who wrote in the latter part of the second century, thus describes the general condition of the Jews in his day :—" Dispersed
and vagabond, exiled from their native soil and
air, they wander over the face of the earth,
without a king, human or divine ; and even as
strangers, they are not permitted to salute with
their footsteps their native land."

Such continued to be their condition until
about A. D. 360, when they were elated with
the prospect of being again restored to their
own country. Julian, the Roman emperor,
having abjured the Christian faith, and wishing
to show his opposition to Christianity, and to
falsify the prediction of Christ respecting Jerusalem, (Luke xxi, 24,) issued an edict for the
rebuilding of the temple, and the restoration

of the Jewish worship in all its original splendour. The whole Jewish world was in commotion. The scattered tribes flocked from the most distant quarters to the holy city, in order to be present and help forward the great national work. Their property, as well as their personal exertions, were freely contributed. The materials for the building were provided, and workmen were already employed in digging the foundations, when, suddenly, flames of fire came bursting from the ground, accompanied with the most frightful explosions. No inducement could prevail on the labourers to continue a work which appeared to excite the anger of Heaven. The enterprise was abandoned as being at once hopeless and impious ; and in the death of Julian, who about the same time was slain in battle by the Persians, the Christian world beheld the vengeance of God, and the Jew the extinction of all his hopes.

Under the successors of Julian, the edict of Adrian against the Jews was renewed, and until the seventh century they durst not so much as come near to bewail the desolation of their city, without first bribing the Roman guards who were placed there to prohibit their approach. Throughout the Roman empire they were deprived of most of the privileges of citizens; their synagogues were frequently destroyed by mobs; they were forbidden by law to celebrate some of their religious festivals; they were restricted in the right of bequeathing their property; and their testimony was not admitted in courts of justice in any cause in which a Christian was interested, not even if a Jew were himself a party in the suit. In the fifth century, the Jews of Alexandria, to the number of about forty thousand, were expelled from the city; their synagogues demolished, and their houses plundered by the populace.*

When Mohammed commenced his career of imposture and conquest, and the valleys of Arabia rung with the triumphant battle-cry of his followers, *The Koran or death!* the Jews of that country were among the first of whom he endeavoured to make proselytes; and failing in his efforts, they became the first victims of his sanguinary teaching. The favour with which he was at first disposed to view them, was, by their persevering refusal to embrace his religion, converted into implacable hatred, with which he pursued them to the last moment of his life. The storm first fell upon a colony of Jews at Medina, who, after defending

* Gibbon's Decline and Fall.

themselves for fifteen days, were compelled to surrender. Mohammed issued immediate orders for a general massacre, and it was with extreme reluctance that he yielded to the importunity of his allies, and consented to spare the lives of his captives. But their property was confiscated, and the wretched band of seven hundred exiles, with their wives and children, were driven out of the country to seek a refuge on the confines of Syria. At another place, seven hundred Jews, who had surrendered at discretion, were dragged in chains to the market place, and there put to death; their wives and children were sold for slaves, and their possessions seized by the conquerors. In one district, the Jewish shepherds and husbandmen were allowed a precarious toleration, being permitted, during the pleasure of the conqueror, to remain and cultivate their grounds on condition of paying *him* one half of the produce: but, in the reign of Omar, the successor of Mohammed, these also were banished the country. The spirit of rancour and hostility which the impostor himself manifested toward the Jews he also infused into the hearts of his followers, who, except where interest prompted a different course, never failed to imitate his example. In all Mohammedan countries no

class of persons have been so universally oppressed and degraded as the unfortunate Jews.
In many parts of the East the tyranny exercised over them is still so severe as to afford
at the present time a literal fulfilment of the
prediction, " *Thy life shall hang in doubt before
thee, and thou shalt have fear day and night, and
shall have none assurance of thy life.*" " For
the murder of a Jew, a Persian has only to cut
around a finger, so as to draw blood, and the
offence is expiated."*

Nor has their condition been more tolerable
in lands that are called Christian. They have
found the adherents of popery as cruel, oppressive, and intolerant, as the followers of the false
prophet, as will be seen by the following account of their treatment in some of the principal countries of Europe.

In SPAIN, Sisebut, who reigned in the beginning of the seventh century, raised a cruel persecution against the Jews, who were then very
numerous in that country, and, having been for
some time tolerated, if not protected, by the
government, appear to have attained a considerable degree of prosperity. But the wealth
which they had accumulated by trade and the

* Alexander's Travels from India to England.

management of the finances, invited the avarice of their masters ; and they might be oppressed without danger, as they had lost the use, and even the remembrance of arms. Ninety thousand Jews were compelled to receive baptism ; the fortunes of those who refused to receive that rite were confiscated, their bodies were tortured, and it seems doubtful whether they were permitted to leave the country. The excessive zeal of the king was moderated even by the clergy of Spain, who declared that baptism ought not to be forcibly administered ; yet, with a singular inconsistency, they decided that those Jews who had already been baptized, should be constrained to observe the outward rites of a religion which they disbelieved and detested.* But this tolerant spirit soon evaporated, and not many years elapsed before the Jews were made the victims of another severe persecution. Laws were enacted, prohibiting, under the severest penalties, the observance of any of the festivals or peculiar rites of Judaism. For observing the passover, the new moon, or the feast of tabernacles, for making a distinction in meats,—for violating the Christian sabbath, or the festivals of the church, either by working in the fields or manufactures,

* Gibbon's Roman Empire.

—the general punishment was one hundred lashes on the naked body; after this the offender was to be put in chains, banished, and his property confiscated to the lord of the soil. They were not allowed to marry without a clause in the act of dower that both parties would become Christians; and all who offended against this law, even the parents concerned in such marriage, were to be fined or scourged. The Jew who read, or allowed his children to read. books written against Christianity, suffered one hundred lashes; on the second offence the lashes were repeated, the offenders banished, and their property confiscated. Several other enactments of a similar character also disgraced these statutes; and if they were not everywhere fully carried into effect, they were only prevented from being so by their extreme and horrible cruelty. A few years after this, the Moors invaded and effected the conquest of Spain, in which they were materially assisted by the Jews, and in consequence, that people were regarded with high favour during the continuance of the Moorish government in that country, which was upward of three hundred years. During this period the Jews rapidly increased in numbers, wealth, and influence. They were the most enlightened class in the kingdom; they were the cultivators and possessors of the soil; they were distinguished for their skill as physicians, and were not unfrequently promoted to high and responsible offices in the state.

On the decay of the Mohammedan power, and the re-establishment of popery, the superior education, the business talents, the wealth and industry of the Jewish population, rendered them too important a class of the community to allow their rights to be rashly interfered with, in a country where the nobles were engaged almost wholly in war, and the lower orders were sunk in the deepest degradation. In the thirteenth century, however, the condition of the Jews began to decline. The superstitions of the people, and the animosities of the priests were bitterly directed against them, and constant attempts were made to encroach upon their rights. They were declared incapable of civil offices; they were compelled to attend a Christian church three times a year; and were required to live in certain specified streets, and thenceforth particular districts were known in every city as the Jews' quarter. These petty annoyances, however, afforded but a feeble presage of the fearful hurricane that at last arose. The attack commenced at Seville, in 1391. The populace, having been incited by a sermon preached in the cathedral by the archbishop, made a general assault upon the Jews' quarter, and of seven thousand families, upward of one half were killed, while the remainder sought safety by a pretended conversion to Christianity. Similar scenes took place in Cordova, Toledo, Valencia, and in all the cities where large numbers of Jews were found. Many thousands were butchered; not a few left the kingdom, seeking a refuge in Italy, Turkey, and the states of Barbary; and it is calculated that two hundred thousand were forced into a profession of Christianity. As soon as the violence of the storm had passed over, many of these new converts relapsed into Judaism, and many more, while they attended the public services of the church, continued to observe in private the usages of their ancient religion. To put an effectual stop to this, the pope issued a bull for the establishment of the inquisition in Spain. This horrible tribunal established its head quarters at Seville; but four inferior inquisitions were also erected in other places. It was invested with power to summon every individual suspected of secret attachment to Judaism; and such was the unsparing severity with which it proceeded, that, in the course of a single year, upward of two thousand persons were put to death in Seville and the immediately surrounding country; several were imprisoned for life, and seventeen thousand suffered lighter punishments. At last a large stone building was constructed for containing a large number of prisoners; combustible materials were laid around the outside of the walls, while the wretched inmates were left to perish by a lingering death. The authority of the inquisition extended only over those Jews who, having professed the Catholic faith to avoid persecution, were suspected of insincerity in their attachment to it. Those who had never renounced Judaism, continued as yet to enjoy comparative security. But their turn soon came. Ferdinand and Isabella, having succeeded in expelling the Moors from Spain, were ambitious of the glory of delivering the land from every taint of heresy. To effect this, nothing was now wanting but the expulsion of the Jews. Accordingly, in 1492 an order was given that every unbaptized Jew should leave the country within four months; all who remained after that period were to be put to death. Upon the issuing of this edict, the minds of the unhappy people were filled with astonishment and horror. From one end of Spain to

the other the voice of lamentation was lifted
up. Every appeal to the justice or mercy of
Ferdinand, or his queen, was alike in vain.
Banishment or conversion were the only alter-
natives. The Jews on this occasion manifested their attachment to their religion by preferring it to every thing else. Upward of three
hundred thousand left all that was dear to them
on earth, and went forth in search of lands
where they might be allowed to worship the
God of their fathers in peace.*

This calamity was considered by the Jews
almost as dreadful as the capture and ruin of
Jerusalem. Misfortune continued to follow the
exiles wherever they went. The account of
their sufferings is heart rending; our limits
permit us only to mention in general, that the
richer part of them withdrew first to PORTU-
GAL, where the Jewish faith had hitherto been
tolerated, and which country they were permitted to enter on paying a toll of eight crusados
a head. But the contagious influence of the
proceedings in Spain soon extended to the sis-
ter kingdom; and the wretched exiles, after
being made the objects of new forms of oppression and injustice, were at last, under circumstances of extreme cruelty, expelled from that

* Encyclopedia Brittannica.

country also. Others, who directed their course to the states of Barbary and Morocco, were subjected to the horrors of shipwreck, famine, and pestilence; some were set ashore on desert islands by the inhuman ship owners, and some were sold as slaves. Some went to Italy, where the hardest fate of all awaited them, in the cruel treatment they met with from their own countrymen, who inhospitably refused to receive them; thousands lay perishing with hunger on the shore, till even the pope [Alex. VI.] interfered by a sentence of banishment against the resident Jews, which was, however, revoked on their paying a considerable sum. But notwithstanding all the sufferings to which they were exposed, and which so considerably diminished their numbers, large communities were formed by the descendants of the exiles in Barbary, Turkey, and Italy. In Spain there were now no professed Jews, nor have they since been tolerated in that country; with the exception of three or four thousand, who reside at Gibraltar, under the protection of Great Britain.

In GERMANY, although the Jews gradually became the objects of aversion to all classes, the protection of the emperors, and the ordinances of the popes, preserved them from gene-

ral attack until the time of the crusades. When
the horde of fanatics, who, in the year 1096,
under the command of Peter the Hermit, commenced the first crusade, were assembled near
Treves, a city on the banks of the Rhine, it
was suggested that before they attempted to
rescue the sepulchre of Christ from the hands
of the infidels, they ought to take vengeance
on those worse unbelievers who had been his
murderers. With one impulse they rushed into
the city. The choice of death or conversion
was given to the miserable Jews, and only a
few escaped the general massacre. Fathers
presented their breasts to the sword, after having slain their own children to prevent their
being brought up as Christians, and the women,
to escape the brutality of the soldiers, fastened
stones to their bodies, and threw themselves
into the river. Similar scenes were repeated
in Cologne, Mentz, Worms, and in all the cities
of the Rhine; and the progress of the armies
was marked by the blood of the Jews, till they
reached the plains of Hungary. Upon a mode-
rate computation, not less than seventeen thousand are supposed to have perished. The
minds of those who escaped were filled with
consternation, and many fled to Siberia, Mora-
via, and Poland. Some, however, still clung

to the land which gave them birth, and fifty years of comparative quiet elapsed for them to multiply again their devoted race, and acquire wealth to undergo their inalienable doom of pillage and massacre. The second crusaders in 1146 attacked them with the same perseeuting spirit as their predecessors; but upon this occasion the greater part saved themselves by a timely flight. A frightful havoc, however, took place among the Jews in the cities of Cologne, Mentz, Worms, Spires, and Strasburg. From the time of the crusades the condition of the Jews in Germany continued unsettled and degraded. History abounds with instances of the injustice which they suffered from the rapacity of the princes, and the tumultuous assaults of the people. From certain states and cities they were interdicted altogether. In others they had a right of residing, and a particular part of the city was assigned them; but they were frequently expelled from the streets to which they had a legal right, in order that a sum of money might be extorted from them for permission to return to their dwellings. The popular fury was ever ready to break out against them, and needy princes held out the threat that unless their coffers were replenished by contributions from the Jews, an incensed populace would be let loose upon them. Upon other occasions the necessity of their conversion was insisted upon, and they were compelled to pay large sums to avoid being forcibly baptized. Enthusiasts arose, who considered themselves commissioned by Heaven to proclaim war against this unhappy people. ·In the thirteenth century, a nobleman, named Rhindfleish, proceeded through many of the most populous towns of Germany, followed by a multitude who destroyed whole communities of Jews. In 1337, a peasant, named Armdler, pursued a similar course, till his atrocities awaked the tardy justice of the emperor, by whom he was put to death. A few years later, when the whole of Europe was desolated by a plague, it was reported in Germany, that the Jews had caused the plague by poisoning the public wells. The effect of this report was terrible. At Basle, the adult Jews were put in a vessel on the Rhine, which was set on fire; the children being spared that they might be educated as Christians. It would be tedious to relate the manner in which the Jews were put to death in other cities; but from Switzerland to Siberia the land was drenched with innocent blood.*

* "About this time, [1349,] the Jews throughout the world were arrested and burned, and their fortunes con-

For some centuries after this, little change was effected in the condition of the Jews in Germany. The laws enacted by Frederick the Great, in 1750, for the regulation of his Jewish subjects, were of the most intolerant description.

In FRANCE, under Pepin, Charlemagne, and their immediate successors, the Jews enjoyed the same protection and privileges as other persons. On account of their superior intelligence and education, they were frequently promoted to offices of trust: they were the physicians, and the ministers of finance to nobles and kings; they engrossed much of the foreign commerce; their vessels crowded the ports, and their merchandize encumbered the quays of the seaports. This state of prosperity continued with little abatement until the tenth century, when the Jews began rapidly to decline from a learned, and influential, and powerful class of the community, to miserable outcasts, the common prey of clergy, nobles, and citizens; and existing in a state worse than slavery itself.

fiscated by those lords under whose jurisdiction they had lived, except at Avignon, and the territories of the church dependant on the pope. Each poor Jew, when he was able to hide himself and arrive in that country, esteemed himself safe."—*Froissart's Chronicles.*

Even in this wretched situation, though deprived of every thing else, and denied the common rights of humanity, they were still possessed of gold. By their loans to the nobles, they had a hold on most of the estates of the country; they had also articles of value in pawn from all classes of the community; even the priests, when in want of money, scrupled not to pledge to them the sacred vessels of the churches. The people were galled by the fact that they stood in the relation of debtor to this despised race; and the usurious interest exacted by the Jews, increased the popular odium against them. In the year 1180, Philip II. issued a decree annulling all debts due to the Jews, and requiring them to surrender all the pledges held by them. A few years after, another edict was issued, which confiscated all their immoveable property, and commanded them immediately to sell all their moveables, and leave the country. Obliged to part with their effects at the lowest prices, they sadly departed, bearing with them little but their destitute wives and children, from the scenes of their birth and infancy. Before twenty years had elapsed, the necessities of the king induced him to allow the Jews, on payment of a sum of money, to re-enter France, which they did in great numbers. The necessities, the cruelty, or superstition of succeeding kings, varied the modes of Jewish persecution. Louis VIII. forbid them receiving interest from their debtors. Louis IX. annulled by law one third of all debts due them; he also published an edict for the destruction of their sacred books [the Talmud] of which twenty-four carts full were burned in the city of Paris. By other laws they were forbidden to hold social intercourse with Christians. In the province of Brittany all debts due to them were annulled; those who held property belonging to them were allowed to retain it; and no punishment could be inflicted on any person for killing a Jew. In 1239, the Jews of Paris, Orleans, and several other cities, were attacked by mobs who committed frightful ravages. To complete their misery, and to mark them out as objects of inevitable persecution, they were compelled to wear a conspicuous brand upon their dress; this consisted of a piece of blue cloth sewed on the front and back of the garment, and was to be worn by both sexes. In France, as in Germany, monstrous reports were circulated of their sacrilege and cruelty. They were accused of throwing poison into the rivers, of practising magic, and of holding correspondence with infidel kings. They were proscribed, plundered, burned to death. In some places they were compelled by torture to confess themselves guilty, and on their confession were burned In other places all Jews were burned without distinction. At Chinon a deep ditch was dug, an enormous pile raised, and one hundred and sixty of both sexes burned together. Those who survived the persecution, purchased their lives by the payment of a large sum of money; and then, as the height of mercy, were permitted to collect the rest of their effects and leave the kingdom. Yet still they sought—even paid a price—to live in a land that oppressed them. Unhappy race! the earth, perhaps, afforded them no safer asylum. Six times were they banished from the country: as many times did they purchase permission to return; but it was only that they might heap up new treasures to become again the victims of avarice and superstition. At length, in the year 1397, during the reign of Charles VI., they were, for the seventh and last time, commanded to quit the kingdom. This sentence was rigidly enforced; the greater part of the exiles withdrew into Germany, Italy, and Poland; and for several centuries after, very few Jews were found in France.

In ENGLAND, though from interested motives they were for a time tolerated by the monarchs, the Jews became objects of popular hatred, partly from superstitious motives, and partly from the odium which was at that time attached to the custom of lending money upon interest, as well as from the rigour with which the practice was exercised by them. They, however, suffered but little, except from the exactions of the sovereigns, until the accession of Richard I. On the coronation of that monarch, some Jews, supposing themselves to be unknown, had incautiously ventured, contrary to an express prohibition, to attend as spectators of the ceremony. Being discovered, an attack was made upon them by the populace, which ended in a general assault upon the Jews. Their houses were broken open and pillaged, and in many instances set on fire. Richard in vain endeavoured to put a stop to the tumult, which continued to rage for two days; and after it had subsided, such was the state of the public feeling, that the government either would not, or dared not, bring to justice those who had been engaged in it. Intelligence of what had been done by the populace of London soon spread through the country, and similar outrages took place in Norwich,

Stamford, and several other towns, in which the Jews were plundered, maltreated, and slain. The country was swarming with soldiers who were preparing to join the crusade to the Holy Land, and who considered themselves justified in robbing the rich Jews, to aid them in their pilgrimage. At York, the Jews took refuge in the castle, and made a vigorous defence; but finding their situation hopeless, they destroyed every thing of value they possessed, cut the throats of their wives and children, set fire to the castle, and then killed themselves. During the two following reigns, the history of England abounds in instances of the oppressions to which the Jews were subject, and of the vast sums extorted from them by the necessities of the monarchs. The tyrannical proceedings of King John toward this unhappy race are well known, and in particular, his ordering that a rich Jew of Bristol should lose a tooth daily till he paid ten thousand marks.* The Jew lost seven teeth before he yielded. Their situation was in no degree improved under Henry III. The superstitions of the people, and the necessities of the government, subjected them to every varied form of contumely and wrong. After the king had repeated his extortions so

* About eighty thousand dollars.

frequently that the Jews made the vain threat of leaving the kingdom, he sold them to his brother for five thousand marks, with full power over their persons and property. At last, in the reign of Edward I., without any known pretext afforded by their conduct, an edict was issued for their expulsion from the country altogether; and after having been deprived of all their possessions, the wretched race, amid the mockery and triumph of the common people, proceeded to the shore, and finally left the island. The number of the exiles amounted to fifteen, or as some say, sixteen thousand. The Jews were not permitted to return to England until the reign of Cromwell, nearly four hundred years after.

The foregoing particulars form but a small portion of the dark catalogue of the calamities and persecutions which have befallen this unhappy race. But enough has been said to show how strikingly the facts of history have corresponded with the language of prophecy. Indeed, it would be scarcely possible to sum up the leading particulars of the Jewish history since the destruction of Jerusalem, in more graphic and forcible language than that of the sacred oracle which predicted their fate:—

" They have been plucked out of their own land, and scattered among all people from one end of the earth even to the other. And among these nations they have had no ease, neither has the sole of their foot had rest ; but the Lord has given them a trembling heart, and failing of eyes, and sorrow of mind. They have been oppressed and spoiled ; their lives have hung in doubt before them ; they have feared day and night, and have had no assurance of their lives."

But there are some further particulars in the prophecy which will require our notice. One of the judgments which Moses denounced against the Jews was, that they should be violently deprived of their children :—*" Thy sons and thy daughters shall be given to another people, and thine eyes shall look, and fail with longing for them all the day long."* When Jerusalem was taken by Titus, all the captives under seventeen years of age, amounting to many thousands, were taken from their parents and sold into slavery. And in modern times, especially in France, Germany, Spain, and Portugal, the children of Jews have often been forcibly taken away and given in charge of the priests, that they might be educated as Christians. When the king of Portugal published the decree for the banishment of the Jews from his kingdom, " he also issued a secret order to seize all the children under fourteen years of age ; to tear them from the arms—the bosoms of their parents, and disperse them through the country, to be baptized and brought up as Christians. The secret transpired, and lest they should conceal their children, it was instantly put into execution."* How great a calamity the Jews considered this, may be judged from the fact, that many parents who were unable to conceal their children, destroyed them with their own hands : frantic mothers threw their infants into wells and rivers, choosing rather to see them perish before their eyes, than fall into the hands of their enemies, to be educated in any other religion than their own.

Moses also predicted that the Jews should become " *an astonishment, a proverb, and a by-word among all nations, whither the Lord should lead them ;*" and Jeremiah declared that they should be " *a reproach, a proverb, a taunt, and a curse in all places.*"† And such has been the case. Among Christians, Mohammedans, and pagans, they have been the objects not only of oppression and persecution, but also of the bitterest

* Millman. † Jeremiah xxiv, 9.

scorn and contempt. Among all nations, the cunning, the avarice, and the usury of the Jews are proverbial ; and their very name has been used as a term of peculiar reproach and infamy. In Spain it was once made a penal offence to call a man a Jew. Mr. Lane informs us that the Egyptians, when quarreling, lavish upon each other the vilest names, such as " son of a dog, pig," and an appellation which they think worse than any of these, namely, " Jew." The same writer also states, that it is common to hear an Arab abuse his jaded ass, and after applying to him various opprobrious epithets, end by calling the beast a Jew.* The emperor Constantine, in a public document, terms the Jews the most hateful of all people.† In most countries they have been without a character or place in society. The very lowest, the dregs of the population, scorned fellowship with them, and avoided them as a contamination. They have been required to live in particular streets, separate from the rest of the inhabitants,‡ and compelled to bear about with them

* Manners and Customs of the Modern Egyptians.
† Rev. H. H. Millman.
‡ That portion of the city of London to which the Jews were formerly restricted still goes by the name of the Old Jewry.

the mark of degradation, and expose themselves to the insults of the populace by wearing a brand on their dress, a cap of a peculiar colour, or some other badge of distinction. In short, they have been

> " Scattered abroad
> Earth's scorn and hissing ; to the race of men
> A loathsome proverb ; spurned by every foot ;
> And cursed by every tongue ; their heritage
> And birthright bondage ; and their very brows
> Bearing, like Cain's, the outcast's mark of hate."

It was foretold that their afflictions should be such that *they should be mad for the sight of their eyes which they should see :*—and what language can better describe the desperation to which they were reduced, and the agony of mind they endured when they were dying of hunger by thousands in the streets of Jerusalem—when they saw their holy temple wrapped in flames, and *felt* that they were forsaken of God—when they slew their wives and children, and afterward killed themselves, to avoid falling into the hands of their ferocious foes—when their children were torn from their arms—when they were stripped of their possessions, and driven as houseless wanderers from the land of their birth, and the homes of their youth, to seek a refuge they knew not whither ? Calamities such as they have endured never yet fell to the lot of any other people.

Finally, it was declared that *their plagues should be wonderful—even great plagues—and of long continuance.* How great and wonderful their plagues have been, we have already shown : but their greatness is not more won derful than their duration. For nearly eighteen centuries have this devoted people " drunk at the hand of the Lord the cup of his fury ; they have drunken the dregs of the cup of trembling, and wrung them out;" and although in most countries their condition is now infinitely supe- rior to what it formerly was, they are still a dispersed and generally despised people ; and in many lands the hand of the oppressor is yet heavy upon them.

What other nation has sufferd so much, and yet endured so long ? Nay, what other nation, except the Arabs, has subsisted a distinct and unmixed people in their own country, so long as the Jews have done while dispersed among all countries ? What principle of vitality has kept them alive under the " great fight of afflic- tion" which they have had to encounter ? What is it that has enabled them to sustain, for ages, such a weight of oppression without being annihilated by it? What but the power and providence of that God who had decreed both their calamities and their continuance? "I will scatter them," said Jehovah, "among the heathen, and will draw out a sword after them. And yet for all that, when they be in the land of their enemies, *I will not cast them away, neither will I abhor them, to destroy them utterly, and to break my covenant with them, for I am the Lord their God,*" Levit. xxvi, 33, 44. "I will sift the house of Israel among all nations, like as corn is sifted in a sieve, *yet shall not the least grain fall upon the earth,*" Amos ix, 9. And again, "I will make a full end of all the nations whither I have driven them: *but I will not make a full end of them,*" Jer. xlvi, 28. The promise of the Eternal was thus pledged for their preservation, and the utmost efforts of the uncircumcised have been unable to effect their destruction. Kings have employed the severity of their edicts, and the hands of the executioner; they have been murdered by thousands in popular tumults, robbed of their property, and bereaved of their children. They have from age to age run through misery and oppression, and torrents of their own blood. Persecution has unsheathed the sword, and lighted the fagot; papal superstition and Mohammedan

barbarity have smote them with unsparing
ferocity; penal statutes, and deep prejudice
have visited on them most unrighteous chas-
tisement; and notwithstanding all, they sur-
vive! Every means has been employed to
exterminate them; all nations have united in
the design of destroying them. Their steps
have been dogged by an ever-following curse;
go where they would they have been despised,
reviled, and trodden under foot. No other people ever suffered the hundredth part of their
calamities, and still they live! "Like the bush
on Mount Horeb, Israel has continued to burn
without being consumed." For nearly eighteen
hundred years have they been dispersed among
the nations, and "left to the mercy of a world
that everywhere hated and oppressed them—
shattered in pieces like the wreck of a mighty
vessel in a storm—scattered over the earth like
fragments upon the waters." "They have had
no temple, no sacrifice, no prince, no certain
dwelling places. Forbidden to be governed
by their own laws, to choose their own magis-
trates, to maintain any common policy; every
ordinary bond of national union and preservation has been wanting; whatever influences
of local attachment, or of language, or manners,
or government, have been found necessary to

the preservation of other nations, have been denied to *them;* all the influences of internal depression and outward violence which have ever destroyed and blotted out the nations of the earth, have been at work with unprecedented strength, for more than seventeen centuries, upon the national Israel, and still the Jews are a distinct and numerous people, unassimilated with any nation, though dispersed among all nations. Their peculiarities are undiminished; their national identity is unbroken."* However remote from their native land, they are still Jews; however distant from each other, they are still brethren. Indeed no people, not even the most settled nation of Europe, have preserved their race so pure and unmixed as have the scattered and wandering Jews. "In France, who can separate the race of the ancient Gauls from the various other people who from time to time have settled there? In Spain, who can distinguish exactly between the first possessors, the Spaniards, and the Goths and the Moors, who conquered and kept possession of the country for some ages? In England, who can pretend to say with certainty which families are descended from the ancient Britons, and which from the Romans, or Saxons, or

* M'Ilvaine's Lectures.

Danes, or Normans? The most ancient and honourable pedigrees can only be traced up o a certain period, and beyond that there is nothing but conjecture and uncertainty."* No such obscurity, however, rests on the descent of the Jews. They may not be able to distinguish the particular tribe to which they belong, but they know certainly that they are the seed of Jacob, the children of Abraham.†

Meanwhile, what has become of those mighty nations who were the rods of Jehovah's anger in chastising the Jews? " Has not the Lord, according to his word, *made a full end of them?* While Israel has stood unconsumed in the fiery furnace, where are the nations that kindled its flames? Where are the Assyrians and the Chaldeans? Their name is almost forgotten; their existence is known only to history. Where is the empire of the Egyptians? The Macedonians destroyed it, and a descendant of its ancient race cannot be distinguished among the strangers who have ever since pos· sessed its territory. Where are they of Mace-

---

* Bishop Newton.

† The distinctive character and preservation of the Jewish nation were also foretold by Baalam when he prophesied that *the people should dwell alone, and should not be reckoned* [or mingled] *among the nations.* Num. xxiii, 9.

don? The Roman sword subdued their kingdom, and their posterity are mingled inseparably among the confused population of Greece and Turkey. Where is the nation of ancient Rome, the last conquerors of the Jews, and the proud destroyers of Jerusalem? The Goths rolled their flood over its pride. Another nation inhabits the ancient city. Even the language of her former people is dead. The Goths!—where are they? The Jews! where are they not? They witnessed the glory of Egypt, and of Babylon, and of Nineveh; they were in mature age at the birth of Macedon, and of Rome; mighty kingdoms have risen and perished since they began to be scattered and enslaved; and now they traverse the ruins of all, the same people as when they left Judea, preserving in themselves a monument of the days of Moses and the Pharaohs, as unchanged as the pyramids of Memphis, which they are reputed to have built." "You may call upon the ends of the earth, and will call in vain for one living representative of those powerful nations of antiquity, by whom the people of Israel were successively oppressed." They have passed away; their shadows alone haunt the world and flicker upon its tablets. But the Jews walk in every street, dwell in every capital, traverse every exchange, and relieve the monotony of the nations of the earth.

> " Empires have sunk, and kingdoms passed away ;
> But still, apart, sublime in misery, stands
> The wreck of Israel ;"

" and should the voice which is hereafter to gather that people out of all lands, be now heard from Mount Zion, calling for the children of Abraham, no less than four millions would instantly answer to the name, each bearing in himself unquestionable proofs of that noble lineage."*

An exact estimate of the number of Jews now living in the world is of course unattainable; but it is generally believed to be nearly equal to what it was in the time of their greatest prosperity, under David and Solomon.† Their preservation in such numbers, for so many centuries, under circumstances of such singular disadvantage, and in defiance of such cruel measures as have been employed against them, can be deemed nothing less than an ex-

* M'Ilvaine's Lectures.

† There are supposed to be about two and a half. millions in Europe ; Asia probably contains one million ; Africa, about six hundred thousand, and America, twenty thousand.

isting, perpetual miracle. " It can be explained by no fortuitous circumstances ; it admits of no evasion ; it stands forth a palpable, bold, unequivocal proof of the superintendence of Providence, the truth of prophecy, and the divine authority of the Bible."

He that " would see a sign," before he will believe the Scriptures, may in the Jews behold " a sign and a wonder," than which none can be greater. Their universal dispersion, their terrible calamities, and their wonderful preservation, are circumstances that find no parallel in the history of other nations : yet every feature in their extraordinary history was distinct ly foretold more than three thousand years ago, and recorded in the oldest book of which the world has any knowledge. The man who after seriously reviewing the history of this " peculiar people," and comparing it with the predictions of Scripture, " will not believe Moses and the prophets, neither will he be persuaded though one arose from the dead."

But will the Jews always continue an outcast wandering race, objects of the world's scorn shut up in darkness and unbelief ? " Is there no balm in Gilead ?" And will " the health of the daughter of Israel" never be " recovered ?"

"Hath God cast away his people ? God forbid!" Rom. xi, 1. Their sorrows shall not last for ever. There are prophecies yet unfulfilled, which "speak better things" respecting them than those of whose truth they have been so long the living witnesses :—

> "Though dimm'd be Israel's glory now—
>   Forlorn but not forsaken—
> Hope doth impart a fervent glow,
>   The breath of prayer to waken,
> That still the bright and morning star
>   May shed a healing ray ;
> The harbinger, to realms afar,
>   Of Israel's happier day."—T. G. NICHOLAS.

Yes; the "God of Abraham" will yet be mindful of the "seed of Abraham." "They shall return, and seek the Lord their God, and David their king; and shall fear the Lord and his goodness in the latter days," Hosea iii, 5. With "the fulness of the Gentiles," shall *they* also be brought in; "*and so all Israel shall be* gospel; and they shall become true worshippers of the God of their fathers, and of "Jesus Christ whom he has sent." "The cross shall then be raised in glory, amid the hosannahs of the people who once raised it in shame and sorrow, amid execrations; and they who rejected Him who was ordained a 'light to lighten the Gentiles, and the glory of his people Israel,' 'shall look on Him whom they have pierced, and mourn' at the deeds of their fa thers, while they rejoice at the grace so undeservedly manifested to themselves."*

It is perhaps scarcely to be wondered at, that so few Jews have hitherto been led to embrace Christianity. The treatment which for centuries they endured, in countries called Christian, was not such as was likely to win them over to the faith of the gospel. Although during this period there were not wanting those who laboured to effect their conversion, yet the influence of their preaching was counteracted by the bitter and persecuting spirit with which 't was enforced. In modern times, the Protestant churches which have so nobly exerted themselves to send the glad tidings of salvation to all nations, have strangely neglected the Jews. Indeed, they would seem almost to

* Fraser's Magazine, Sept., 1840.

have considered them as a people " given over to a reprobate mind," whose conversion it was hopeless to attempt or desire. While " sea and land" have been " compassed to make proselytes," and the heralds of the cross have been despatched to China and Greenland, to India and Greece, to the far off isles of the sea, and to lands

" But little noticed, and of little note,"

comparatively few have been found to care for the souls of that people to whom were first " committed the oracles of God," and " of whom, as concerning the flesh, Christ came." But we trust that " another spirit" is about to animate the churches. The case of the Jews is awakening an interest which it never before excited ; and many a pious heart is beating in unison with that of the apostle when he exclaimed, " My heart's desire and prayer to God for Israel is, that they might be saved," Romans x, 1.

extended beyond the original design of the writer, yet he cannot refrain from making a few extracts from the report which the deputation, on their return, presented to the general assembly of the Scottish Church.

At Smyrna, which contains several thousand Jews, one of the deputation unexpectedly entering the house of a respectable Jewish family, surprised a young man in the act of reading the New Testament. The gentleman expressing his delight at finding him thus engaged, inquired his opinion of the book he had been reading. He replied, " It is the best book in the world, and the Old Testament is the next best." When asked why he did not openly avow himself a Christian, he replied, that imprisonment and banishment would be the immediate consequence of his doing so ; but if these restraints were removed, he and several other young men in Smyrna would publicly embrace Christianity.

At Pest, the capital of Hungary, Dr. Keith, one of the deputation, was detained by ill health longer than he intended. This city contains upward of eleven thousand Jews, and the doctor says,—" There are at least three thousand who wholly disregard the Talmud, and renounce the superstition and mummery of the synagogue.* They have a simple form of worship; the master preaches to the congregation, which consists of from fifteen hundred to two thousand, on their own sabbath, from the texts of the Old Testament. It is the easiest thing to discuss with them the Messiahship of Jesus. There are inquirers from time to time. One aged Jew said, ' O, it is a hard thing to renounce opinions which have been believed from youth as undoubted.' If I had remained a few weeks longer at Pest, every hour of the day some inquiring Jew would have come to ask respecting Christ.—The number of Jews in Hungary is two hundred and fifty thousand, at the lowest estimate, and some rate them at double that number. This is a place in which,

* The Jewish rabbins pretend that besides the written law, God communicated to Moses many other laws and regulations which were not committed to writing, but transmitted orally from one generation to another, and hence called " the tradition of the elders." The *Talmud* is a collection of these traditions, with a commentary upon them, and is an immense work, comprising several folio volumes. Many of its requisitions are frivolous and absurd, and others profane and unscriptural, yet the rabbins teach, and most of the Jews believe, that it is of equal, if not superior authority to the Bible. For a further account of it, see Prideaux's Connections, Clarke's Commentary on Matthew xv, 2, and Watson's Dictionary, page 531.

according to inquiry, there are promising openings for a mission to the Jewish nation ; to them the simplicity of the gospel is altogether unknown ; as yet they know nothing of the gospel but from the corruptions of the Greek and Roman Churches ; and yet conversions are made from year to year. If the Jew can be converted to such a faith, O, may he not be led rather to Jesus Christ, without shocking his natural feelings at the idolatry of the Gentiles ? Shall the call be in vain ? It is for the general assembly—it is for the church of Christ to answer."

Another of the deputation reports, that " the London Society for the Conversion of the Jews have an interesting and effective mission in the south of Palestine, its head quarters being Jerusalem." He further states that " it is the testimony of Professor Tholuck [of Germany] that since the beginning of the present century more Jews had been brought to the knowledge of the Christian faith than during all the centuries preceding from the death of Christ. One of the ministers of Berlin said he had baptized with his own hand, of late years, one hundred and twelve Jews."

To the present improved condition of the Jews in a temporal view, we have already

adverted, [page 128.] In most countries of
Europe they are not only free from persecution, but receive the same protection from the
laws, and enjoy nearly the same privileges as
other citizens. Every succeeding year seems
to bring with it some additional proof of their
altered circumstances, and of the diminution of
Gentile prejudices. Increase of kindly feeling
on the part of Christians toward the Jews will
naturally produce some degree of reciprocal
feeling on their part, and dispose them to a
more favourable investigation of the claims of
Christianity. From various accounts it appears that in several places a spirit of religious
inquiry is already awakened among them; that
the Talmud, which has hitherto been the greatest obstacle to their conversion, is fast falling
into disrepute; and that, weary of waiting for a
Messiah who has so long disappointed their
expectations, many are beginning to ask among
themselves whether "he that should come," has
not already appeared. Under these circumstances may we not hope, that even now the
day of their "redemption draweth nigh," and
that "the veil" which "is upon their heart" is
about to be "taken away?" 2 Cor. iii, 15, 16.
Surely, if missionaries possessing the requisite
qualifications were to go among them, like the

apostles of old, "visiting from house to house," and "preaching in the synagogues," showing to them from their own "Scriptures that Jesus is Christ," the unbelief which has hitherto been proof against both the force of argument and the argument of force, would yield to the influence of *truth spoken in love.* As Christians, we owe the Jews a debt of gratitude which can never be fully repaid. To them, instrumentally, we are indebted for the Scriptures, not only of the Old, but also of the New Testament; for "the glorious company of the apostles," as well as "the goodly fellowship of the prophets" were Jews. We ought, then, to do at least as much for *them* as we do for those nations who have no *special* claims upon us. "Pray for the peace of Jerusalem."

"Have they stumbled that they should fall? God forbid : but through their fall salvation is come unto the Gentiles, for to provoke them to jealousy.—For as ye [Gentiles] in times past have not believed God, yet have now obtained mercy through their unbelief: even so have these also now not believed God, *that through your mercy they also may obtain mercy.* Now, if the fall of them be the riches of the world, and the diminishing of them be the riches of the

Gentiles; how much more their fulness?—If
the casting away of them be the reconciling of
the world, what shall the receiving of them be
but life from the dead?" Rom. xi, 11, &c.

> "Father of faithful Abraham, hear
>   Our earnest suit for Abraham's seed;
> Justly they claim the softest prayer
>   From us, adopted in their stead,
> Who mercy through their fall obtain,
> And Christ by their rejection gain.
>
> Outcasts from thee, and scatter'd wide,
>   Through every nation under heaven,
> Blaspheming whom they crucified,
>   Unsaved, unpitied, unforgiven;
> Branded like Cain, they bear their load,
> Abhorr'd of man, and cursed of God.
>
> But hast thou finally forsook,
>   For ever cast thy own away?
> Wilt thou not bid the murderers look
>   On Him they pierced, and weep, and pray?
> Yes, gracious Lord, thy word is past;
> All Israel shall be saved at last.
>
> Come then, thou great Deliverer, come,
>   The veil from Jacob's heart remove:
> Receive thy ancient people home!
>   That, quicken'd by thy dying love,
> The world may their reception find,
> Life from the dead for all mankind."

CHARLES WESLEY.

CHAPTER V.

PROPHECIES CONCERNING THE HOLY LAND.

Interesting associations of this land—Its situation, extent, and character—Prophecies respecting it—Were partially fulfilled during the Babylonish captivity—More fully accomplished after its subjection by the Romans—Present state of the country agrees with the prophecies—The land is desolate—Testimony of Sandys, Volney, Maundrell, Addison, Hardy, Jowett, Burckhardt, and Joliffe—The highways are desolate—Extracts from Hardy, Volney, Richardson, Jowett, and Addison—The cities are waste—Ruinous state of the ancient cities and towns as described by modern travellers—Flourishing condition of Galilee in the time of Josephus—Contrast exhibited in its present state—Scripture accounts of the former populousness and abundance of the Holy Land, doubted by some writers—Confirmed by the positive testimony of history, and by the present indications of the country—Testimony of Gibbon and Volney to these facts—Remarkable verification of Scripture prophecy, from Volney's Ruins—Unfulfilled prophecies of the restoration of the Jews, and the future prosperity of the Holy Land—Poem.

WE have shown in the two preceding chapters how literally and fearfully have been accomplished the threatenings of Jehovah against the disobedient Jews. We will now proceed to exhibit the fulfilment of those prophecies which refer to their ancient country: for the judgments of the Lord were not pronounced against the people only: God " cursed the ground" also, for their sakes; and the land in which they dwelt was, equally with themselves,' the object of prophetic denunciation.

10

There is no other spot on the face of the earth that is regarded by the Christian with feelings of such intense interest and curiosity as the Holy Land. Every portion of its varied territory, its mountains, its valleys, its lakes, its rivers, and even its deserts, are rendered sacred in his eyes, by some deeply interesting association. There it was that Jehovah established the commonwealth of Israel, inspired his prophets, sent angels to converse with men, and manifested his power and his presence in a peculiar manner. There the worship of the one true God was preserved and perpetuated for more than fifteen centuries; for "in Judah was God known, and his name was great in Israel," while all the rest of the world was sunk in the grossest superstition and idolatry.

"Blest land of Judea! thrice hallow'd of song,
  Where the holiest of memories pilgrim-like throng,
  In the shade of thy palms, by the shores of thy sea,
  On the hills of thy beauty, my heart is with thee.

  With the eye of a spirit I look on that shore
  Where pilgrim and prophet have linger'd before;
  With the glide of a spirit I traverse the sod
  Made bright by the steps of the angels of God."
                                        WHITTIER.

But, above all, this land is hallowed as be-

-ing the place which was honoured by the per
sonal ministry of the Messiah—the Son of God.

" Here his blessing was heard, and his lessons were taught,
Here the blind was restored, and the healing was wrought,"

and here he accomplished the mystery of man's
redemption by the offering of himself as an
atonement for the sins of the world.

This interesting country—the scene of Scripture history, the theatre of miracle and of prophecy—lies on the eastern shore of the Mediterranean Sea, which forms its western boundary, between the thirty-first and thirty-fourth
degrees of north latitude. It is bounded on the
north by the mountains of Lebanon ; on the
south by the deserts of Arabia ; and on the east
by the desert of Syria and the Dead Sea.

As early as the time of Abraham, this favoured spot was designated by God as the chosen
residence of his " peculiar people." " To thee
will I give it, and to thy seed for ever," was
the promise of Jehovah respecting it, to that
patriarch. Nor was it unworthy of the distinction thus conferred upon it ; for although inconsiderable in point of extent, being only about one
hundred and eighty miles long, with an average
breadth of not more than seventy, yet such
was the salubrity of its climate and the fertility

of its soil, that it was not only abundantly capable of supplying the wants of its inhabitants, even when most densely peopled, but also furnished a large surplus of corn which they disposed of to the Phenicians of Tyre and Sidon. 1 Kings v, 11; Ezek. xxvii, 7; Acts xii, 20. "It had enough of mountain, and stream, and lake, and sea, to render it complete in its own resources;" while the natural barriers, with which it was surrounded on all sides, rendered it easy of defence against foreign invasion. "Nor must it be forgotten, that its position, almost in the centre of the three great continents of Europe, Asia, and Africa, was the most desirable that could have been chosen 'when the fulness of time was come,' and the blessings of revelation and redemption were to be scattered among the dwellers upon earth."*

The general appearance and character of the country were thus accurately described by Moses to the children of Israel while on their way thither:—"The land whither thou goest in to possess it, is not as the land of Egypt, from whence ye came out, where thou sowedst thy seed and wateredst it with thy foot, as a garden of herbs: but the land whither ye go to possess it, is a land of hills and valleys, and

* Hardy.

drinketh water of the rain of heaven.—For the Lord thy God bringeth thee into a good land, a land of brooks of water, of fountains, and depths that spring out of valleys and hills; a land of wheat, and barley, and vines, and fig-trees, and pomegranates; a land of oil-olive, and honey; a land wherein thou shalt eat bread without scarceness, thou shalt not lack any thing in it," Deut. viii, 7–9; xi, 10, 11.

The abundant supply of water is thus prominently mentioned, " as being the most important circumstance in an oriental country, where its value is incalculable. Only one who has travelled in the East, and knows practically the astonishing difference between a watered and unwatered country, can enter into the full force of this foremost characteristic of the Promised land. The reader who looks on a general map will see at a glance that there is no country in Western Asia more liberally supplied with streams of water. The benefit of these streams is incalculable, although, as is the case in those regions with all streams of no considerable magnitude, they are [except the Jordan] rather winter torrents than rivers."*

Unlike Egypt, which is exceedingly plain and level, Canaan was diversified with hills

* Pictorial Bible

and valleys, which not only added to the beauty
of the scenery, but also, by varying the tempe-
rature of the country, rendered it capable of
producing the fruits of the most distant cli-
mates.   Under the sway of the Canaanites it
brought forth in such abundance, that even the
spies sent by Moses, while they endeavoured
to dissuade the Israelites from attempting to
possess it, were constrained to say concerning
it, "It is a good land which the Lord our God
doth give us," Num. xiii, 27; Deut. i, 25.   In
other parts of Scripture it is called "the pleasant land," Psa. cvi, 24; Zech. vii, 14; "the
glory of all lands," Ezek. xx, 6; and in many
places it is termed "a land flowing with milk
and honey."

Such then was the country which God gave
to Israel for a possession :—

"A land of corn, and wine, and oil,
   Favour'd with God's peculiar smile,
    With every blessing blest."

But its glory and abundance were to continue
only so long as the Israelites remained faithful to their covenant with God.   Before they
set foot on their promised inheritance, Jehovah, by the mouth of his servant Moses, thus
solemnly warned them of the consequences of
violating his commands :—

" If ye walk contrary unto me, and will not hearken unto me, I will bring seven times more plagues upon you according to your sins. —And your highways shall be desolate; and I will make your cities waste, and bring your sanctuaries into desolation.—And I will bring the land into desolation: and your enemies which dwell therein shall be astonished at it. And I will scatter you among the heathen, and I will draw out a sword after you, and your land shall be desolate, and your cities waste. Then shall the land enjoy her sabbaths,* as long as it lieth desolate, and ye be in your enemies' land; even then shall the land rest, and enjoy her sabbaths," Levit. xxvi, 21, 22, 31-34. " The generation to come of your children that shall rise up after you, and the stranger that shall come from a far land, shall say, when they see the plagues of that land, and the sicknesses which the Lord hath laid upon it; and

* *The land shall enjoy her sabbaths*—that is, it shall lie waste and uncultivated. The expression has reference to that injunction of the Mosaic law by which the Jews were forbidden to cultivate the ground every seventh year; this year was called " the sabbath of the land," because in it the land had rest. During this sabbatical year the people were to subsist on the superabundance of the preceding year, in which the ground produced a treble crop. Leviticus xxv, 2-7, 21, 22.

that the whole land thereof is brimstone, and salt, and burning,* that it is not sown, nor beareth, nor any grass groweth therein, like the overthrow of Sodom and Gomorrah, Admah and Zeboim, which the Lord overthrew in his anger, and in his wrath : even all nations shall say, 'Wherefore hath the Lord done this unto this land ? What meaneth the heat of this great anger ?' Then men shall say, 'Because they have forsaken the covenant of the Lord God of their fathers, which he made with them when he brought them out of the land of Egypt,'" Deuteronomy xxix, 22-25.

The faithful warnings of Moses being disregarded by the Jews, Jehovah, in after times, sent other prophets unto them, " rising up early and sending them, and saying, 'Turn ye from the evil of your doings, and dwell in the land that the Lord hath given to you and to your

* These expressions are not to be understood literally, being only strong figures of speech to denote extreme desolation and barrenness ; and in this way they are still used in the East. Mr. Roberts, in his Oriental Illustrations, says, "When a place is noted for being unhealthy, or the land very unfruitful, it is called *kenthago poomy*, a place or country of brimstone. Trincomalee, and some other places, have gained this appellation on account of the heat and sterility of their soils."

fathers for ever : and go not after other gods to serve them, and provoke me not to anger with the work of your hands ; and I will do you no hurt.'—Yet they obeyed not, nor inclined their ear, but walked every one in the imagination of their evil heart ;" and in consequence thereof, the Lord has brought upon their country " all the curses which were written" in his book " concerning" it.

This was accomplished, first, when Judah was carried away captive by Nebuchadnezzar, at which time the land lay desolate seventy years. Jeremiah, the " weeping prophet," thus mournfully describes the affliction of the land at this period :—

" How hath the Lord covered the daughter of Zion with
　　a cloud in his anger,
And cast down from heaven unto the earth the beauty
　　of Israel,
And remembered not his footstool in the day of his anger !
The Lord was an enemy : he hath swallowed up Israel,
He hath swallowed up all her palaces ;
He hath destroyed her strong holds,
And hath increased in the daughter of Judah mourning
　　and lamentation.
The Lord hath cast off his altar,
He hath abhorred his sanctuary,
He hath given up into the hand of the enemy the walls
　　of her palaces.
He hath destroyed and broken her bars ;

Her king and her princes are among the Gentiles.
All that pass by her clap their hands,
They hiss and wag their head at the daughter of Jeru-
salem,
Saying, ' Is this the city that men call the perfection of
beauty, the joy of the whole earth !'
Our inheritance is turned to strangers,
Our houses to aliens.
For this our heart is faint ;
For these things our eyes are dim ;
Because of the mountain of Zion which is desolate,
The foxes walk upon it.
The crown is fallen from our head ;
Wo unto us, that we have sinned !"

LAM. ii, 1, 5, 7, 9, 15 ; v, 2, 17, 18, 16.

But the predictions of Moses were more especially fulfilled in the judgments visited upon
Judea and its inhabitants by the Romans, and
the almost perpetual desolation of the country
since that period.   While the Jews are now in
their " enemies' land," suffering the punishment
of their sins, the actual state of their own land,
as it now is, and for many centuries has been,
exactly corresponds with the prophecies delivered by their leader and lawgiver, upward
of three thousand years ago.

of history, and of every traveller who has visited the country. In the first and second centuries, Palestine was devastated by the wars with the Romans, until the country was literally converted into a desert. It continued subject to the power of Rome until it was seized upon and laid waste by the Arabian tribes collected under the banner of Mohammed. It was after this torn in pieces by the civil wars between the two rival sects of Mohammedans, wrested from the caliphs by their rebellious governors, taken from them by the Turcoman soldiers, several times invaded by the European crusaders, retaken by the mamalukes of Egypt, ravaged by Tamerlane and his Tartars, and at last reduced to subjection by the Turks.

It is easy to conceive the lamentable condition of a country almost depopulated by a series of desolating wars, frequently changing masters, and at length falling under the dominion of a wretched and tyrannical government like that of Turkey, which, while it has strength sufficient to oppress the miserable inhabitants, and deprive them of the fruits of their industry, is yet unable to protect them from the hordes of wandering Arabs who people the surrounding deserts, and to whose predatory incursions they are continually exposed.

" Thus mourn, beneath the oppressor's rod,
The fields where faithful Abraham trod,
Where Isaac walk'd by twilight gleam,
And heaven came down on Jacob's dream."
                                    J. MONTGOMERY.

To the desolate condition of the land all travellers bear witness. Sandys, in 1610, speaking of Palestine and the adjacent lands, says,—
" These countries, once so glorious and famous
for their happy estate, are now, through vice
and ingratitude, become the most deplored spectacles of extreme miserie. Those rich lands
at this present remaine waste and overgrowne
with bushes, receptacles of wild beasts, of
theeues and murderers ; large territories dis-
peopled or thinly inhabited ; goodly cities made
desolate ; sumptuous buildings become ruines ;
glorious temples either subverted or prostituted
to impiety ; true religion discountenanced and

to the supply of their necessary wants. The husbandman only sows to keep himself from starving. The condition of the peasants is miserable. The art of cultivation is in the most deplorable state; the husbandman is destitute of instruments, or has very bad ones; his plough is frequently no more than the branch of a tree, cut below a bifurcation, and used without wheels.—In the mountains they do not prune their vines, and they nowhere ingraft trees.—In the districts exposed to the Arabs, as in Palestine, the countryman must sow with his musket in his hand. Scarcely does the corn turn yellow, before it is reaped, and concealed in *matmoures*, or subterranean caverns. As little as possible is saved for seed corn, because they sow no more than is barely necessary for subsistence; in a word, their whole industry is limited to a supply of their immediate wants; and to procure a little bread, a few onions, a wretched blue shirt, and a bit of woollen, much labour is not necessary." At the conclusion of his work, he says, that after having lived for some time in these " once flourishing and populous, but now desolate and barbarous countries," he could not, on his return to France, avoid feeling a kind of surprise, when, " instead of those ruined countries and vast deserts," to which he had been accustomed, he found himself in a well-cultivated and populous territory.

Maundrell, when journeying southward from Nablous, the ancient Shechem, observes,—"All along this day's travel from Kane Leban to Beer, [which lies about ten miles north of Jerusalem,] and also, as far as we could see around, the country presents nothing to the view in most places but naked rocks, mountains, and precipices, at sight of which pilgrims are apt to be much astonished and balked in their expectations; finding that country in such an inhospitable condition, concerning whose pleasantness and plenty they had before formed in their minds such high ideas, from the description given of it in the word of God." Of the once fertile plain of Jericho he says, it is now "extremely barren, producing nothing but a kind of samphire and other marine plants; and in many places where puddles of water had stood in the road, we observed a whiteness on the ground, which we found to be a crust of salt, raised by the water out of the earth." Of weeds, which at the time when we passed it were as high as the horses' backs."

Burckhardt states, that "the greater part of the valley of the Jordan is a parched desert, of which a few spots only are cultivated by the Bedouins.

Of the celebrated plain of Esdraelon, where the tribe of Issachar "rejoiced in their tents," and whose soil is the richest of any in Palestine, Mr. Addison says,—"After riding among undulating hills for about an hour, we entered the broad flat plain of Esdraelon. It is silent and solitary over its wide extent, presenting an appearance very similar to the desert plains leading to Palmyra. It possesses a most fertile soil ; and the rich black mould, parched and dusty, was covered with a dense and luxuriant crop of thistles and weeds. In no part of the wide surface of this lifeless plain could a tree be seen, a single village, a single town, a single cultivated enclosed field, or a solitary human habitation." Mr. Hardy remarks, that "the soil is in some places more than six feet thick, and exceedingly rich, and were the plain well cultivated, it would be one of the most productive in the world. It is about fifty miles long, and twenty broad." He observed "a few small villages scattered over its surface but not perhaps a hundredth part of the number it is well able to sustain." Dr. Clarke terms it " a solitude," and compares it to " a vast meadow covered with the richest pasture." Mr. Jowett says,—" We counted, in our road across the plain, only five very small villages, consisting of wretched mud hovels, chiefly in ruins. On this noble plain, if there were perfect security from the government,—a thing now unknown for centuries,—where we saw but five small villages, twenty-five good towns, each with a population of one thousand souls, might stand at a distance of three miles from each other."

Mr. Joliffe, writing from Jerusalem, says,— " From the centre of the neighbouring elevations is seen a wild, rugged, and mountainous desert ; no herds depasturing on the summits, no forests clothing the acclivities, no waters flowing through the valleys ; but one rude scene of melancholy waste, in the midst of which the ancient glory of Judea bows her head in widowed desolation." " All around Jerusalem," says Dr. Richardson, " the general aspect is blighted and barren ; the grass is withered ; the bare seems in doubt whether to come to maturity or die in the ear."

Mr. Hardy says,—" In looking at some of the barren hills of Judea, where the beast wanders not, the bird flies not, and the grass grows not, I have seen the impress of the curse of God, in more dreadful characters than are to be seen elsewhere on this side the grave; a sight rendered still more striking by the beautiful flowers, and the patches of flourishing grain, that here and there present themselves, as if to show what the land was once, and what it again may be, when the blessing of the Lord shall rest upon the city and upon the field, and the labour of man's hand be refreshed by the former and latter rain."

The highways shall be desolate.—There have probably been few countries between the various parts of which there was so frequent and regular an intercourse as in Palestine, while inhabited by the children of Israel. Three times every year were all the males, from every part of the country, required, by the precepts of their law, to present themselves before the Lord in Jerusalem, on which occasions they were not unfrequently accompanied by their wives and families. Deut. xvi, 16;

11

Luke ii, 41–44.   On the recurrence of these periodical pilgrimages, the "highways,"—thronged with persons of all ages and of both sexes —old men and venerable matrons, the time of whose departure was at hand, young men rejoicing in their strength, and the daughters of Israel blooming in youth and beauty—some journeying on foot, others travelling by the various modes of conveyance used in those days —must have presented a spectacle of the most picturesque and animated character.   But now, how changed the scene !   " The paths are deserted where the tribes once approached from the most distant parts to the festivals of the temple."*   " The ways of Zion do mourn because none come to her solemn feasts.—The highways lie waste, the wayfaring man ceaseth."   " In the interior parts of Syria there are neither great roads, nor canals, nor even bridges over the greatest parts of the rivers and torrents, however necessary they may be in winter.   Between town and town there are neither posts nor public conveyances.—Nobody travels alone, from the insecurity of the roads.   One must wait for several travellers assumes the office of protector, but is more frequently the oppressor of the caravan. These precautions are, above all, necessary in the countries exposed to the Arabs, such as Palestine.—It is remarkable, that we never see either a wagon, or a cart, in all Syria."* " Among the hills of Palestine, the road is impassable, and the traveller finds himself among a set of infamous and ignorant thieves, who would cut his throat for a farthing, and rob him of his money for the mere pleasure of doing it."†

Mr. Jowett, speaking of his journey across the great plain of Esdraelon, says,—" We saw very few persons on the road ; we might truly apply to this scene the words of Deborah,— *The highways were unoccupied,*" Judges v, 6, 7. In another place he remarks,—" From the window of the khan where we are lodging, we have a clear view of the tract over which Elijah must have passed, when he girded up his loins, and ran before the chariot of Ahab to the entrance of Jezreel. 1 Kings xviii, 44–46. But in the present day, no chariots are to be seen— not even a single wheel carriage of any description whatever.—The roads among the mountains are so neglected—such mere single foot paths —that it is difficult to imagine in what way cha-

* Volney.   † Dr. Richardson.

riots could now convey the traveller to Jerusalem, or over the chief part of the Holy Land."

"What a contrast," observes Mr. Addison, " does the present aspect of the land bear to its past state! Where are now the towns and villages mentioned in the Roman itineraries, the numerous ' *viæ publicæ*,' or public highways therein enumerated, and the population and productions of time past, when ' the land was full of.horses, neither was there any end of chariots,' Isa. ii, 7.—There is now no such thing as a carriage or chariot in the whole country, nor a single carriage road."　　*

Your land shall be desolate, and your cities waste.—The one was the necessary result of the other. The country being desolate and uncultivated, its ancient cities, once so numerous, powerful, and populous, as a natural and an inevitable consequence, have fallen to decay.

JERUSALEM, once " beautiful for situation, the joy of the whole earth," is now nothing more than an ordinary Syrian town of the third or fourth class, with a population of not more than from twelve to fifteen thousand. "This filled up, and all its buildings embarrassed with ruins, we can scarcely believe we view that celebrated metropolis which formerly withstood the efforts of the most powerful empires, and, for a time, resisted the arms of Rome herself; —in a word, we with difficulty recognise Jerusalem." "Jerusalem," says Mr. Hardy, "is one of the dullest places I ever entered;—it has lost its rank in political importance—there is now no higher power than a delegated governor, who is a person of comparatively low rank." Dr. Olin tells us that a large number of the houses are in a dilapidated and ruinous condition; and that nearly the whole population are in a state of the most abject poverty and wretchedness, the result of oppression, the absence of trade, and the utter stagnation of all branches of industry.

" How doth the city sit solitary, that was full of people !
How is she become as a widow !
She that was great among the nations,
And princess among the provinces,
How is she become tributary !
From the daughter of Zion all her beauty is departed ; ··
Her children are gone into captivity before the enemy ;—
For the Lord hath afflicted her for the multitude of her
transgressions."   LAM. i, 1, 5, 6.

SAMARIA, the capital of the short-lived and wicked kingdom of Israel, is reduced to almost complete desolation. This city was beautifully situated. It occupied the summit of a large, well-shaped, oval hill, surrounded by a fruitful valley, and enclosed on all sides by hills equally beautiful. " It would be difficult," says Dr. Robinson, " to find in all Palestine a situation of equal strength, fertility, and beauty combined. In all these particulars it has very greatly the advantage over Jerusalem." Concerning this place the following prophecies were delivered :—

"Samaria shall become desolate ;
　For she hath rebelled against her God."—Hos. xiii 16.
"I will make Samaria as a heap of the field,
　And as plantings of a vineyard :
　And I will pour down the stones thereof into the valley,
　And I will discover the foundations thereof.—Mic. i, 6.

Samaria was taken, after a seige of three years, by the king of Assyria. 2 Kings xvii, 5, 6. Josephus (Ant. b. xiii, c. 10) tells us that it was again taken, after a seige of one year, by John Hyrcanns, who razed it to the ground. It was rebuilt, and strongly fortified, by Herod, who gave it the name of Sebaste. The present appearance of the place shows the literal fulfilment of tire site, except the small spot on the eastern slope occupied by the miserable village which still retains the name of Sebaste.—*Olin*—*Maundrell.*

JERICHO, which in the time of Christ was second only to Jerusalem, is so utterly destroyed that the precise spot where it stood is now matter of speculation. The village of Rihah, long but erroneously supposed to occupy its site, is spoken of by Dr. Olin and others as one of the meanest in Palestine. BETHEL, now called Beitin has been deserted for ages. " Its ruins," says Dr. Robinson" cover a space of three or four acres. They consist of very many foundations and half-standing walls of houses and other buildings. A few Arabs had pitched their tents here for the summer, to watch their flocks and fields of grain; and they were the only inhabitants." From the same authority we learn that Seilun, the ancient SHILOH, is a desolation covered with ruins of comparatively modern date, among which are many large stones and fragments of columns, shewing it to have been an ancient site. Of BETHSHAN "the only remains are large heaps of black hewn stones, many foundations of houses, and the fragments of a few columns; the present village, called Bysan, contains about seventy or eighty houses, and the inhabitants are in a miserable condition from being exposed to the

depredations of the Bedouins."—*Burckhardt.*
LYDDA, now called Ludd, described by Josephus as being not inferior in size to a city, has, says Volney, "the appearance of a place lately ravaged by fire and sword. From the huts of the inhabitants to the palace of the Aga is one vast heap of rubbish and ruins." ARIMATHEA has so utterly passed away that its site is now unknown; and so also of many other once flourishing cities.

CESEREA, the once splendid city of Herod, exhibits an awful contrast to its former magnificence, by the present desolate appearance of its ruins. Not a single inhabitant remains; jackals and beasts of prey, with a few birds and lizards, are the only living possessors of this once crowded city.—*Clarke—Hardy.*

Dr. Robinson, travelling in the "hill-country" of Judea, says, "Many of the hills were marked with ruins, showing that this tract of country was once thickly inhabited:" and again, "The country is full of sites of ruins," &c.

Josephus says of Galilee,—"The country is rich and fruitful, and is all cultivated. Moreover the cities lie here very thick; and the very many villages that are here, are everywhere so full of people, by the richness of the soil, that the very least of them contains above fifteen thousand inhabitants." What a contrast does this descrip-

tion present to the present condition of·this territory. There is not now in all Galilee a single
city containing more than six thousand inhabitants ; and the numerous cities which then
studded the shores of its beautiful lake, have,
with the single exception of Tiberias, long
been abandoned to utter desolation. "When,"
observes Mr. Addison, "we survey the silence
and solitude of these shores, and cast our eyes
over the expanse of water, whose blue surface
is checkered by no boat or sail, we are led to
draw a vivid and melancholy comparison between the past and present state of this now
solitary region. Along this wide-extended line·
of coast, now so silent and deserted, once stood
the flourishing and populous cities of MAG-
DALA, BETHSAIDA, CHORAZIN, CAPERNAUM, &c.
In the ruined harbours, and in the lone and
solitary bays which extend around the deserted
sites of these once flourishing cities, bustling
fleets of boats and vessels, whether for peace
or war, were fitted out. Now no boat is to be
seen upon its waters, and no trace of man upon
its shore, except where a few flat-roofed houses,
a few palm trees, two solitary minarets, and
the dome of a little mosque, close to the water's
edge, marked the little town of Tabareah, the
humble representative of the ancient Tiberias."

In the country beyond Jordan are the desolate remains of several ancient cities. The ruins of Djcrash, supposed from its situation and the similarity of the name to be the ancient Gerasa, are of the most magnificent character, and prove the former magnitude and importance of that city.*

Of the many populous and extensive cities with which, in the days of its prosperity, the Holy Land was so thickly settled, there are now we beleive, only four that contain over five thousand inhabitants: these are Jeruslem, Hebron, Saphet, and Nablous, (the ancient Shechem,) the three latter of which are computed to contain each a population of about six thousand souls.

"When we survey the present deplorable state of this country, the poverty of the villages, the scantiness of the population; and when we cast our eyes over the sites of the ruined cities, and regard the crumbling fabrics of past times mouldering to pieces, the towering column and the sculptured stone half covered by the burying sand,"† what a mournful contrast do we witness to the time when the land, " flowing with milk and honey," was the " glory of all lands;" when it was also " full of silver and gold, and there was no end of its treasures," and Jcrusa-

* Burckhardt.   † Addison.

lem, its metropolis, was "the joy of the whole earth!" What a wonderful attestation does it furnish of the truth of Scripture prophecy! "The land is a witness as well as the people. The Israelite in our streets, whose appearance was delineated with such graphic precision by the legislator prophet more than thirty-three centuries ago, is not a surer evidence of the inspiration of the sacred volume," than the general desolation, and almost depopulation, of the land in which they formerly dwelt.

Indeed, so striking is the general aspect of poverty, desolation, and barrenness which this region now exhibits, that some writers have adduced it as an objection to the truth of Scripture, affirming that so barren, wretched, and inconsiderable a country could never have been the pleasant and fruitful land which the sacred writers represent it to have been, or have sustained the immense population which are said to have inhabited it. But these ob- jectors are either ignorant or forgetful that the present desolation of the Holy Land was dis- tinctly foretold by the prophets; and therefore, so far from being an objection to the truth of the Bible, it is, on the contrary, a strong con- firmation of it; while its ancient fertility and populousness, which they affect to deny, is

established by evidence, independent of Scripture, which can neither be gainsayed nor refuted.
Of the province of Galilee, Josephus says, in
addition to what we have already quoted, [page
168,] that "its fruitfulness was such as to
invite the most slothful to take pains in its cultivation." Of the provinces of Judea and Samaria, he tells us that " they are each of them
very full of people, which is the greatest sign
of excellence and abundance."* Tacitus, the
Roman historian, who, it should be remembered, was strongly prejudiced against the
Jews, speaking of their country, says,—" The
soil is rich and fertile ; besides the fruits
known in Italy, the palm and balm tree flourish
in great luxuriance."†

"Those," observes Mr. Wilde, " who ex-
claim against the infertility and barrenness of
this country, should recollect that want of cultivation gives it much of the sterile and barren
appearance which it now presents to the traveller. The plough used in that country is
one of the rudest instruments of any implement
of the kind I have seen. It does little more
than scratch the soil, making a furrow scarcely
three inches deep." We cannot fairly judge
of its former capabilities by its present con-

* Wars, book iii, chap. 3.   † Hist., book vi, sec. 6.

dition. Successively wasted by the Romans, Saracens, and crusaders, and then falling under the iron yoke of Turkish despotism, and exposed to hordes of plundering Arabs, it is impossible that it should now present the appearance of fertility and abundance which it anciently did. Yet even under these unfavourable circumstances it still exhibits such manifest tokens of its former productiveness and high state of cultivation, as to enable the traveller to "discover without difficulty that this fine country was not surpassed in beauty and exuberant production by any country of Western Asia."* "The fruits," remarks Mr. Joliffe, "surpass in richness any thing that I have elsewhere met with." "Were good government, good faith, and good manners to flourish in this land for half a century, it would literally become again a land flowing with milk and honey."† "Under a wise and beneficent government," observes Dr. Clarke, "the produce of the Holy Land would exceed all calculation. Its perennial harvest,‡ the salubrity of its air, its limpid springs, its rivers, lakes, and matchless plains, its hills and vales,—all these, added to the serenity of its climate, prove this

* Pictorial Bible.   † Jowett.
‡ Levit. xxvi, 5 ; Amos ix, 13.

land to be indeed *a field which the Lord hath blessed.*" Speaking of a portion of the country then under the sway of a comparatively mild governor, he says,—" It was pleasing to observe the effects of better government ;—the cultivation was everywhere marvellous ;—the hills, from their bases to their summits, were entirely covered with gardens ; all of these were free from weeds, and in the highest state of agricultural perfection.—A sight of this territory can alone convey any adequate idea of its surprising produce."* Even the most barren and rugged mountains are capable of cultivation, and were anciently made to contribute greatly toward the support of a large population. From the base to the summit they were hewed into terraces, which were covered with soil. Upon these they "planted the fig, the olive, and the vine, and sowed corn, and all kinds of pulse, which, favoured by the usual spring and autumnal rains, by the dew which never fails, by the warmth

* The doctor here speaks of the country between Nablous and Jerusalem. Its short-lived prosperity, however, passed away with the government of the pacha under whom it arose ; and this region now presents the same desolate aspect which it did when visited by Maundrell, whose description of it is given on page 158.

of the sun, and the mild climate, produced the finest fruit, and most excellent corn."[*] Traces of this kind of cultivation are still to be seen in the mountainous districts of the Holy Land, and are mentioned by almost every traveller.[†]

By no writers is the former excellence of this country more positively asserted than by Gibbon and Volney, men whose devotion to the cause of infidelity was so notorious that none will suspect them of being influenced in their statements by any prejudices in *favour* of divine revelation. The former says,—" Syria, one of the countries that have been improved by the most early cultivation, is not unworthy the preference. The heat of the climate is tempered by the vicinity of the sea and mountains, by the plenty of wood and water ; and the produce of a fertile soil affords the subsistence, and encourages the propagation of men and animals. From the age of David to that of Heraclius, the country was overspread with ancient and flourishing cities."[‡] Volney, after estimating the number of inhabitants in Syria, observes,—" So feeble a population, in

* D'Arvieux.
† Maundrell, Shaw, Volney, Clarke, Hardy, Jowett, &c
‡ Decline and Fall, chap. 51.

so excellent a country, may well excite our astonishment; but this will be still increased if we compare the present number of inhabitants with that of ancient times. We are informed by the philosophical geographer, Strabo, that the territories of Jamnia and Joppa in Palestine, alone, were formerly so populous, as to be able to bring forty thousand armed men into the field. At present they could scarcely furnish three thousand. From the accounts we have of Judea in the time of Titus, and which are to be esteemed tolerably accurate, that country must have contained four millions of inhabitants; but at present there are not, perhaps, above three hundred thousand.* If we go still further back into antiquity, we shall find the same populousness among the Philistines, the Phœnicians, and in the kingdoms of Samaria and Damascus." After stating that some writers have called in question these facts, he proceeds to show the fallacy of their objections; and then he adds,—"There is nothing in nature or experience to contradict the great population of high antiquity: without

---

* The word "Judea," as used by Volney in the above statement, must be understood as including the whole of Palestine, and not merely the Roman province of Judea, which comprised only the southern section of the country.

appealing to the positive testimony of history, there are innumerable monuments which depose in favour of the fact. Such are the prodigious quantities of ruins dispersed over the plains, and even in the mountains, at this day deserted. On the most remote parts of Carmel are found wild vines and olive trees, which must have been conveyed thither by the hand of man; and in Lebanon, the rocks now abandoned to fir trees and brambles, present us in a thousand places with terraces, which prove they were anciently better cultivated, and consequently much more populous than in our days." Thus the Scripture accounts of the ancient fertility and populousness of the Holy Land are fully confirmed, both by the testimony of history, and the present indications of the country, " even our enemies themselves being judges."

It was predicted that the desolation of the country would be such as to excite the astonishment of those who should witness it. "The generation to come of your children, and *the stranger that shall come from a far land, shall say,* when they see the plagues of that land, *Wherefore hath the Lord done thus unto this land? What meaneth the heat of this great anger?"* More than three thousand years after these words were spoken, Volney, a distinguished traveller, but a professed infidel, and a scoffer at the Scriptures, visits this smitten country. He is *a stranger from a far land.* Deeply impressed with the melancholy aspect of every thing around him, he exclaims,— " The history of past times strongly presented itself to my thoughts.—I enumerated the kingdoms of Damascus and Idumea ; of Jerusalem and Samaria ; and the warlike states of the Philistines ; and the commercial republics of Phœnicia. This Syria, said I to myself, then contained a hundred flourishing cities, and abounded with towns, villages, and hamlets. Everywhere one might have seen cultivated fields, frequented roads, and crowded habitations. Ah ! what are become of those ages of abundance and of life ? What are become of so many productions of the hand of man ?— Alas ! I have traversed this desolate country, I have visited the places that were the theatre of so much splendour, and I have beheld nothing but solitude and desertion. I looked for those ancient people and their works, and all I could find was a faint trace, like to what the foot of a traveller leaves on the sand. The temples are thrown down, the palaces demolished, the ports filled up, the towns destroyed; and the earth, stripped of its inhabitants, seems a dreary burying place.—Great God! *from whence proceed such melancholy revolutions? For what cause is the fortune of these countries so strikingly changed? Why is not that ancient population reproduced and perpetuated?"** This remarkable verification of a Scripture prophecy occurs in a work written with the avowed design of overthrowing the religion of the Bible. How truly is it said, "HE maketh the wrath of man to praise Him!"

Thus have the threatened judgments of the Lord been visited upon the inheritance of Israel. *The land is brought into desolation,—the highways are desolate,—the cities are waste.*

> "To hill and mountain the devouring curse
>   Hath clung; and rivers down unpeopled vales
>   Like mournful pilgrims glide."

And this state of desolation, we are assured, is to continue so long as the Jews "are in their enemies' land," Levit. xxvi, 34. "Thus there may almost be said to be a kind of sympathetic feeling between the bereaved country

---

* Volney's Ruins, chap. 2.

and its banished people;" the land, lying desolate, mourns the absence of her children, awaits
their return, and refuses to be comforted till
they are restored to her. And they *shall* be
restored. The " sure word of prophecy" hath
declared it. "The mouth of the Lord hath
spoken it." Even the very terms of the threat-
ening,—" the land shall enjoy her sabbaths,
while she lieth desolate without them,"—indicate that a period shall arrive which will terminate at once the dispersion of the people, and the
desolation of the country. The same prophecy
also expressly declares that if the people shall
confess their iniquity, and humble their hearts,
then the Lord will "remember his covenant
with Abraham, and Isaac, and Jacob," and will
also " remember the land," Gen. xvii, 7, 8, 19;
xxviii, 14; Levit. xxvi, 40–45.

The writings of the later prophets abound
with predictions of the restoration of the Jews
to their own land. It is true that these predictions were delivered previous to their return from
the Babylonish captivity, and that the greater
part of them were spoken with especial reference to that event; but still there are many
which were not, and could not have been, fulfilled at that time, and must, therefore, refer to
a restoration which is yet to come. Such is

the promise contained in Isaiah lxi, 4, where it is said,—

"They shall build the old wastes,
  They shall raise up the former desolations,
  And shall repair the waste cities,
  The desolation of many generations."

These words cannot refer to the return of the Jews from Babylon, for they were not there "many generations :" indeed, some of the very individuals who were carried there at the commencement of the captivity lived to return to Jerusalem, and witness the founding of the second temple.   Ezra iii, 12.

The return of the Jews from Babylon was but a *partial* one ; the great body of the people did not return to their own land.   But Ezekiel (xxxix, 25–30) foretels a restoration so complete that there shall be "none of them left among the heathen."   This prophecy, therefore, yet remains to be fulfilled.

There are other prophecies in which the return of the Jews to their own land is connected with their subjection to the kingdom of the Messiah.   Thus in Ezekiel xxxiv, 11–13, 23, it is said,—

"Thus saith the Lord God ;
  Behold, as a shepherd searcheth out his flock
  In the day that he is among his sheep that are scattered ;

So will I seek out my sheep,
And will deliver them from all places whither they
    have been scattered.
And I will bring them out from the people,
And gather them from the countries,
And will bring them to their own land,
And feed them upon the mountains of Israel.
And I will set up one Shepherd over them,
And he shall feed them,
Even my servant David;
He shall feed them, and he shall be their Shepherd."

A prediction of similar import is found in Ezekiel xxxvii, 21, 24, 25.

"I will take the children of Israel from among the hea-
    then whither they be gone,
And will gather them on every side,
And bring them into their own land.
And David my servant shall be King over them,
And they shall have one Shepherd;
And they shall dwell in the land that I have given to
    Jacob my servant,
Wherein your fathers have dwelt,
And they shall dwell therein for ever;
And my servant David shall be their Prince for ever."

These predictions, as Dr. A. Clarke* observes, can refer only to the times of the Messiah, who is here intended by the terms Shepherd, and David, which are also applied

---

* See his notes on these passages, and on the parallel texts.

to him in other passages, both of the Old and New Testaments.* So, also, they are under-stood by the Jewish rabbins, who, in these prophecies, read, instead of "David," *Messiah the son of David.* David, king of Israel, had at this time been dead upward of four hundred years, and there has never since been a ruler of any kind, either in the Jewish church or state, of that name. Moreover, the Jews have been *no nation* since the return from Babylon; they are no nation now; and it is only in the *latter days* that they can expect to be a *nation*, and that must be a *Christian nation.* We are obliged, therefore, from the evidence of these *prophecies*,—from the evidence of the above *facts*,—from the evidence of the *rabbins* themselves,—and from the evidence of the *New Testament*, to consider these texts as applying to JESUS CHRIST, the promised MESSIAH, who has been a *light to lighten the Gentiles*, and will yet be the *glory of his people Israel.*

That they shall again be restored to the country of their ancestors, is the universal expectation of the Jews themselves. They

* Isa. lv, 3, 4; Jer. xxx, 3–11; Hosea iii, 4, 5; Matt. xii, 23; xxi, 9; John x, 14–16; Heb. xiii, 20.

song is unchangeable :—

> "If I forget thee, O Jerusalem, let my right hand forget her cunning.
> If I do not remember thee, let my tongue cleave to the roof of my mouth ;
> If I prefer not Jerusalem above my chief joy." '
>
> PSALM cxxxvii, 5.

"No matter what the station or rank ; no matter what, or how distant, the country where the Jew resides, he still lives upon the hope that he will some time journey Zionward."* But ere this takes place, they must abandon their fallacious hopes of a future Messiah, and acknowledge as their Saviour and Redeemer him whom their fathers rejected and crucified. Then may they expect the fulfilment of their dearest wishes—the realization of their long-cherished hopes. "An exile of eighteen centuries has not extinguished the heaven-chartered title of the 'seed of Abraham' to the final and everlasting possession of the Promised Land." Gen. xvii, 7, 8. The word of the Lord

* Wilde.

concerning Zion, which he hath neither forgotten nor forsaken, is,—

> "Behold I have graven thee upon the palms of my
>   hands ;
> Thy walls are continually before me.
> Thy children shall make haste ;
> Thy destroyers and they that made thee waste shall go
>   forth of thee." Isa. xlix, 14–23.

God will "remember the land," and gather together unto it his ancient people. From the thousand lands in which they are scattered shall the weary-footed wanderers direct their steps toward the home of their fathers ; " and the ransomed of the Lord shall return, and come to Zion with songs and everlasting joy upon their heads." They shall build up the waste places of Jerusalem, and inhabit again the mountains of Israel. " The wilderness and the solitary place shall be glad for them ; and the desert shall rejoice and blossom as the rose. It shall blossom abundantly, and rejoice even with joy and singing : the glory of Lebanon shall be given unto it, the excellency of Carmel and of Sharon.—Violence shall no more be heard in their land, wasting nor destruction within their borders ; but they shall call their walls Salvation, and their gates Praise. The people also shall be all right-

eous; and they shall inherit the **land for**
ever.—I THE LORD WILL HASTEN IT IN HIS
TIME."

"And she, being desolate, shall sit upon the ground."—Isa. iii, 26.

> Who is this that mournful sits
>   Beneath the palm tree's shade?
> To the conqueror stern submits,
>   In trophied pride array'd?
> None sustains the head depress'd,
>   None the word of comfort speaks!
> Lo, her sorrows soil her breast,
>   Her tears are on her cheeks!
>
> Ah! it is Zion in captivity
>   That thus sits desolate!
>   Her sad estate

Who but will join in deep lament,
With thy sad sons in banishment?
Who will not mingle tears with thine,
Defiled, deserted Palestine?
While o'er the scene of thy solemnities
  They turn their wond'ring eyes,
  And see the Gentile there,
  Where once thy house of prayer
Received the radiance of the orient skies.

Ye who love the sacred land
  To ancient Israel given,
Ye who seek to understand
  The mysteries of heaven,
Listen to the raptured tones
  Of Zion's loftiest lyre,
Form, with Abraham's favour'd sons,
  One sweet harmonious choir.
From each respondent comes the strain,
  That He who in disdain
Disown'd Jerusalem,
  Will yet recall her to his arms again.

Her sons shall from the dust arise,
Hear the heralds of the skies,
Hail with joy Messiah's name,
Him the Prince of life proclaim,
Loud, though late, hosannas raise,
Christ, the son of David, praise.

Then shall the Lord his ancient word fulfil;
  To David's head the regal crown restore;
Again his temple build on Zion's hill;
  Replant his vine, to root it out no more.

Israel's mountains then shall bear
    The withering curse no more ;
Truth and justice ruling there
    The blessing shall restore.

The sacred land, now desolate,
Shall then regain its lost estate ;
Then shall the towers of Zion stand secure ;
    Her bright foundations sure,
Reflecting heaven's own beams, shall evermore endure.

Haste, then, ye days of glory, when the light
    Now beaming from the star of prophecy
Shall fade, absorb'd in perfect vision bright :
    When Zion's watchmen, seeing eye to eye,
    From all her walls shall shout salvation nigh :
        When with the herald's voice
        Re-echoing wilds rejoice,
And loud winds waft it to the listening sky.

                              MRS. BULMER.

CHAPTER VI.

PROPHECIES RESPECTING AMMON AND MOAB.

The Ammonites and Moabites descended from Lot—Were noted for their hostility to the Jews—Prophecies respecting the AMMON-ITES—The Ammonites as a nation are perished—Contrast between the fate of the Ammonites and that of the Jews—The country of Ammon until recently but little known—Desolation of Rabbah foretold—Fulfilment of this prediction—Testimony of Seetzen, Burckhardt, Buckingham, and Lord Lindsay—General desolation of the country—Prophecies respecting MOAB—The Moabites carried captive by Nebuchadnezzar—Are destroyed from being a people—Their country desolate and almost uninhabited—Their ancient cities ruined and deserted—Many of these ruined sites still retain their ancient names—Conclusion.

" I WILL make of thee," said Jehovah to Abraham, " a great nation ; and I will bless him that blesseth thee, and I will curse him that curseth thee," Gen. xii, 2, 3. The latter part of this prediction is strikingly illustrated by the fate of the various nations which at different times have risen up againt the Jews " to do them hurt."

Among these we find the Ammonites and Moabites, who were the descendants of Ben-ammi and Moab, the two sons of Lot. Gen. xix, 37, 38. Both of these nations were gross idolaters, and were distinguished for their enmity to the Hebrews, embracing every opportunity to harass and oppress them. They refused them a passage through their country when on their journey from Egypt to Canaan, and likewise hired Balaam to curse them, but God turned his curse into a blessing. Deut. xxiii, 3–5. In the time of the judges they invaded and subdued the land of Israel, and oppressed the people for eighteen years. Judges iii, 12–14. In the reign of David, however, they were in their turn conquered by the Israelites, and remained in a state of subjection, paying tribute to the kings of Israel, until after the death of Ahab, when they revolted, (2 Kings iii, 4, 5,) and though afterward several times defeated, they do not appear to have been ever again entirely subdued. They acted as the auxiliaries of Nebuchadnezzar when he invaded Judea in the reign of Jehoiakim. They reviled and insulted the Jews when Judea was laid waste, and profanely exulted over the destruction of Jerusalem, and the desecration of the temple. For this, as well as for their general wickedness, the judgments of the Lord were pronounced against them. Isa. xvi, 6–14; Jer. xlviii; xlix, 1, 2; Ezek. xxv, 1–10; Amos i, 13–15; Zeph. ii, 7–10.

The prophecies respecting these nations are of a kindred character, and have been most literally fulfilled. We will first notice those which refer to the land and people of

AMMON.

"The word of the Lord," saith Ezekiel, "came unto me, saying, Son of man, set thy face against the Ammonites, and prophesy against them; and say unto the Ammonites, Hear ye the word of the Lord God; thus saith the Lord God,—

'Because thou saidst, Aha, against my sanctuary, when it was profaned;
And against the land of Israel, when it was desolate;
And against the house of Judah, when they went into captivity;
Behold, therefore, I will deliver thee to the men of the east for a possession,
And they shall set their palaces in thee,
And make their dwellings in thee:
They shall eat thy fruit, and they shall drink thy milk.
And I will make Rabbah a stable for camels,
And the Ammonites* a couching-place for flocks:

* By the word "Ammonites," we must of course understand the chief city or cities of the Ammonites, for it is not expressive of desolation that flocks should pasture anywhere in the open country; but it is eminently so, that they should be stabled among the ruins, and fed upon the sites of cities once populous and flourishing. That this is the sense is shown by the context, as well as by other passages.—*Pictorial Bible.*

And ye shall know that I am the Lord.
Behold, I will stretch out mine hand upon thee,
And will deliver thee for a spoil to the heathen;
And I will cut thee off from the people,
And I will cause thee to perish out of the countries;
I will destroy thee ; and thou shalt know that I am the
    LORD.' "   ·   EZEK. xxv, 1–7.

From these predictions, and from some others of a similar import, (Zeph. ii, 7–10,) it will be seen, that the Ammonites were to perish as a nation—that Rabbah, their capital, was to be utterly ruined—and their country to become desolate.

I will cut thee off from the people—I will cause thee to perish out of the countries—I will destroy thee.—The Ammonites suffered in common with the neighbouring nations, when Nebuchadnezzar invaded Judea and the adjacent countries, and carried the inhabitants into captivity, but, as was foretold by Jeremiah, (xlix, 6,) they were, on the subversion of the Babylonish empire, permitted to return to their own land. After this we find them exposed to the various revolutions with which the people of Syria and Palestine were visited, being sometimes subject to the kings of Egypt, and sometimes to those of Syria.   During the persecutions of the Jews by Antiochus Epiphanes, the Ammonites exercised great cruelties against such of them as lived in their parts: in consequence of this they were attacked by Judas Maccabeus, who defeated them in several battles, and took the city of Jazer, with the adjoining towns.* This was their last conflict with the descendants of Israel; their power was broken, and from this period they rapidly declined, until at length, in accordance with the prophecy, they became extinct as a nation. They were gradually blended with the Arabs, and Origen, who lived in the fourth century, assures us that in his days they were only known under this general name.

There is in this particular a striking difference between the fate of the Ammonites and that of the Jews. The latter, though they have for many centuries been dispersed among all nations, have survived to this day as a distinct people; and their renowned land has never, since they left it, ceased to be known and regarded with interest, because they once occupied it. But for ages the existence of the Ammonites as a nation, or even as a tribe, has been extinct; none are now called by their name, nor do any claim a descent from them. And as to their

* 1 Maccabees v, 1–8; Josephus, Ant., book xii, chap. 8, sec. 1.

13

country, it has only been within the last few years that it has been noticed by European travellers, or that any information concerning it has been acquired. Till then its situation generally was collected from Scripture intimations, which, with some information from ancient writers concerning its towns, formed the amount of what was known respecting the land of Ammon. And even now, while the antiquarian traveller knows that he is in that land, recognises the names which the Bible has made familiar, marks the position and character of sites and ruins, and, whether he intends it or not, collects information to confirm the truth of Scripture prophecy,—the few inhabitants, while they preserve the names which the Ammonites gave to their towns, have no traditions concerning that people, nor do they know whose land it is that they occupy. So utterly is the memory of the Ammonites perished, that it would at this day be unknown that such a people ever existed, or that the country in question was ever in their possession, were it not that the sacred book preserves the record of their history and doom.* They are " cut off from the people," and are " no more remembered among the nations."

* See Pictorial Bible, note on Ezek. xxv 7–10.

I will make Rabbah a stable for camels, and the Ammonites a couching-place for flocks. Ammon shall be a perpetual desolation.—The precise and striking manner in which the prophecies respecting this city have ›en accomplished, gives the place more interest than it could historically claim, although even that is not inconsiderable. Rabbah, called also Rabbath-ammon, was a city of great antiquity, having been the capital of the Ammonites before the Hebrews entered the land of Canaan. It was taken from the Ammonites by David, (2 Sam. xii, 26–29,) but when the tribes beyond Jordan were carried into captivity, the Ammonites regained possession of the cities which had been taken from them.

Although Rabbah appears to have been several times wholly or partially destroyed in war, by the kings of Babylon, and the Greek monarchs of Syria and Egypt, yet the successive conquerors, down to the time of the Romans, appear to have rebuilt and improved the city, being sensible of its advantageous situation, so that it very long maintained its rank as the local metropolis. From Ptolemy Philadelphus, by whom it was restored and fortified, it received the name of Philadelphia, but some of the ancient writers continued to call it by its old name. The character of some of its existing remains shows that the place was improved and embellished while possessed by the Romans; but after their time it seems to have lost its consequence, although the date of its final desolation is unknown. In the time of Jerome it still subsisted under the name of Philadelphia. The Orientals, however, preserve old names with remarkable tenacity, and the ruined city of the Ammonites is still called *Amman* by the natives of the country. The researches of Seetzen, Burckhardt, Buckingham, G. Robinson, and Lord Lindsay, have made us fully acquainted with this site, concerning which we had previously no information. The principal ruins lie along the banks of a small river, called *Moiet Ammon*, [the water of Ammon,] and occupy an area formed by the openings of two valleys. At the point where the valleys meet, and commanding the entrance, there is a high hill, on the summit of which are the remains of a strong and extensive fortress—almost a town in itself—the walls of which are formed of huge blocks of stone, resting one upon another, without any cement, and appear to be of very remote antiquity.*

* This was probably the strong hold which Joab wished David to have the honour of taking, after he had himself

Although this town has been destroyed and deserted for many ages, there are still some remarkable ruins which attest its ancient splendour. Among these, Seetzen and Burckhardt enumerate a square building, highly ornamented, which has been, perhaps, a mausoleum; the ruins of a large palace; a magnificent amphitheatre of immense size, and well preserved; a temple with a great number of columns; the ruins of a large church; the remains of a temple with columns set in a circular form, and which are of extraordinary size; the remains of the ancient wall, with several other edifices. Burckhardt further states, that a large portion of the site is " covered with the ruins of private buildings—but nothing of them remains, except the foundations and some of the door posts." When Mr. Buckingham visited Rabbath-ammon, he halted for the night with a tribe of Arabs, who were found encamped among the ruins, in a hollow behind the top of the threatre. Next morning he makes the following remark in his journal :—" During the night I was almost entirely prevented from sleeping, by the bleating of the flocks, the neighing of mares, and the barking of dogs." He also describes, among

taken the lower town, which he calls "the city of waters."—*Pictorial Bible.*

the ruins, a building surrounding " an open square court, with arched recesses on each side. The recesses in the northern and southern walls were originally open passages, and had arched doorways facing each other; but the first of these was found wholly closed up, and the last was partially filled up, leaving only a narrow passage, just sufficient for the entrance of one man, and of the goats which the Arab keepers drive in here occasionally for shelter during the night."

The latest account of Rabbah is that given by Lord Lindsay, who thus describes it :— " We descended a precipitous stony slope into the valley of Ammon, and crossed a beautiful stream,* bordered at intervals by strips of stunted grass, often interrupted; no oleanders cheered the eye with their rich blossoms; the hills on both sides were rocky and bare, and pierced with excavations and natural caves. Here, at a turning in the narrow valley, commences the antiquities of Amman. It was situated on both sides the stream. The dreariness of its present aspect is quite indescribable—it looks like the

* The Moiet Ammon. It has its source in a pond a few hundred paces from the south-west end of the town, and after passing under ground several times, empties itself into the Jabbok.

abode of death; the valley stinks with dead camels; one of them was rotting in the stream; and although we saw none among the ruins, they were absolutely covered in every direction with their dung. That morning's ride would have convinced a skeptic. How runs the prophecy?—'*I will make Rabbah a stable for camels, and the Ammonites a couching-place for flocks; and ye shall know that I am the Lord!*' Nothing but the croaking of frogs, and screams of wild birds broke the silence, as we advanced up this valley of desolation.—It was a bright, cheerful morning, but still the valley is a very dreary spot, even when the sun shines brightest. Vultures were garbaging on a camel, as we slowly rode back through the glen, and reascended the *akiba* by which we entered it. Amman is now quite deserted except by the Bedouins, who water their flocks at its little river. We met sheep and goats by thousands, and camels by hundreds, coming down to drink, all in beautiful condition."

When the prophets of Israel pronounced the doom of Rabbah, more than a thousand years had given uninterrupted experience of its stability; for a thousand years has it now lain desolate; yet still it is not so utterly extinct but that the Bedouin, who alone frequents the spot, can fold his cattle in its temples and palaces, fulfilling the divine prediction, that the proud Rabbah of the Ammonites should be " a stable for camels, and a couching-place for flocks."

The whole country also partakes of the same desolate character. Mr. G. Robinson says,— "To the southward of the river Zerka (the Jabbok of the Scriptures) commences the country anciently inhabited by the Ammonites ; a country in those days as remarkable for its rich productions, as for the number and strength of the cities which covered its surface. It is now one vast desert, having long since ceased to be inhabited by man in a civilized state." It consists of a series of extensive plains, having a rich soil, but exhibiting no traces of cultivation Mr. Buckingham, viewing one of these plains from an eminence, observes,—"Throughout its whole extent were seen ruined towns in every direction, both before, behind, and on each side of us ; generally seated on small eminences, all at a short distance from each other ; and all we had yet seen bearing evident marks of former opulence and consideration. My guide, who had been over every part of it, assured me that the whole plain was covered with the finest soil, and capable of being the most productive corn land in the world. It is true that for the space of thirty miles there did not appear to me a single interruption of hill, rock, or wood, to impede immediate tillage ; and it is certain that the great plain of Esdraelon, so justly celebrated for its extent and fertility, is inferior in both to this plain. Like Esdraelon, it appears also to have been once the seat of an active and numerous population." " While numerous ruins indicate how rich and populous the country once was, it is now without fixed inhabitants. The wandering tribes resort to it in the summer months, for the sake of the pasturage which it offers ; but when they have left, the ashes and dung of their encampments are the only signs of human occupation which the country affords. Thus truly has Ammon become " a desolation," as the prophets foretold."*

We now pass on to the prophecies respecting

MOAB,

which are more numerous, and equally explicit.

" Against Moab, thus saith the Lord of hosts,
Wo unto Nebo ! for it is spoiled ;
Kiriathaim is confounded and taken ;
Misgab is confounded and dismayed.

* Pictorial History of Palestine.

The spoiler shall come upon every city,
And no city shall escape;
The valley also shall perish,
And the plain shall be destroyed.
Give wings unto Moab,
That it may flee and get away:
For the cities thereof shall be desolate,
Without any to dwell therein.

    Moab hath been at ease from his youth,
And he hath settled on his lees;
And he hath not been emptied from vessel to vessel,
Neither hath he gone into captivity.
Therefore, behold the days come, saith the Lord,
That I will send unto him wanderers that shall cause
    him to wander.
Thou daughter that dost inhabit Dibon:
Come down from thy glory and sit in thirst,
For the spoiler of Moab shall come upon thee,
And he shall destroy thy strong holds.

    Moab is confounded; for it is broken down;
Howl and cry;
Tell ye it in Arnon, that Moab is spoiled.
And judgment is come upon the plain country;
Upon Holon, and upon Jahazah, and upon Mephaath,
And upon Dibon, and upon Nebo,
And upon Kerioth, and upon Bozrah,
And upon all the cities of Moab, far or near.
And joy and gladness is taken
From the plentiful field, and from the land of Moab.
And Moab shall be destroyed from being a people,
Because he hath magnified himself against the Lord."

JER. xlviii.

"Moab shall be a perpetual desolation." ZEPH. ii, 9.

These predictions began to be accomplished when Nebuchadnezzar, five years after the destruction of Jerusalem, invaded Moab and carried away its inhabitants ; thus, according to the prophecy, *causing to wander* from their home, the people who had never before " gone into captivity." Although they were probably permitted to return to their own land when Cyrus overthrew the kingdom of Babylon, yet it does not appear that they were ever again an independent nation. They were successively subject to the Persians, Syrians, Egyptians, and Romans ; and have now, like their brethren the Ammonites, long since been *destroyed from being a people;* their very name was lost, many centuries ago, and they have become mingled with the Jews and Arabians.

Respecting the land and cities of Moab, the prophecies are remarkably full and explicit, but not more so than the evidence of their complete fulfilment, which the present state of that country furnishes.

Moab shall be a perpetual desolation. The valley shall perish, and the plain shall be destroyed.—The land of Moab lay on the eastern side of the Dead Sea, to the south, and partly to the north, of the river Arnon. The surface of the country is more diversified with hill and dale than is that of the Ammonites, further east. The valleys, through which streams flow at all times of the year, are generally beautifully wooded. Although the land now lies desolate, and the sand and salt of the desert and the Dead Sea encroach upon its borders, there is not wanting abundant evidence of its ancient fertility and numerous population. The land thus desert is eminently fertile in its natural character, and continues to afford rich returns in the few spots which are under cultivation. The extraordinary number of ruined towns, often in close proximity to each other, testify that the ancient populousness of this region was in full accordance with the rich character of the soil. The country may now be said to be abandoned, except by a few wandering and hostile Arab tribes, who pasture their flocks on the wild herbage of its once cultivated plains. Vestiges of the ancient field enclosures may still be traced; and there are remains of ancient highways, which in some places are completely paved, and in which there are milestones of the time of Trajan, Aurelius, and Severus, with the number of the miles still legible upon them. These latter facts show that the land of Moab continued to be populous and cultivated, down to a period considerably subsequent to that in which the canon of Scripture was closed.*   There could, therefore, in the times of the prophets, have been no probability that it would ever be reduced to that state of utter desolation " in which it has continued for so many ages, and which vindicates to this hour the truth of Scripture prophecy."

The cities shall be desolate, without any to dwell therein.   The spoiler shall come upon every city, no city shall escape.—We have already adverted to the ancient populousness of the land of Moab.   There are few modern countries so thickly covered with inhabited towns as Moab is with ruined and deserted ones. The accounts of this region were, until the early part of the present century, uncommonly meagre; "for, through fear of the predatory Arabs by whom it is frequented, none of the numerous travellers in Palestine ventured to explore it. ˙ Seetzen, who, in February and March, 1806, not without danger of his life, undertook a tour from Damascus down to the south of Jordan and the Dead Sea, and thence to Jerusalem, was the first to shed a new and altogether unexpected light upon the topogra-

* Pictorial Bible—Irby and Mangles—Burckhardt.

phy of this region, and thereby upon our prophecy. He found a multitude of places, or at
least ruins of places, still bearing the old
names."* Since that period it has been visited
by several other travellers. Burckhardt mentions the names of forty ruined sites, which
he passed in the course of his route through
this country. Messrs. Irby and Mangles tell
us, " the whole of the plains are covered with
the sites of towns, on every eminence or spot
convenient for the situation of one." Among
the ruins are the remains of temples, sepulchral
monuments, and other edifices. In some of the
buildings are stones twenty feet in length, and
so broad that one constitutes the thickness
of the wall. Many of these sites of ruins still
bear names corresponding to those by which
the cities of Moab are designated in Scripture.
Burckhardt says,—" The ruins of Eleale, Heshbon, Meon, Medeba, Dibon, and Aroer, all
situated on the north side of the Arnon, still
subsist, to illustrate the history of the children
of Israel.† To the south of the wild torrent
Modjeb [Arnon] I found the considerable ruins

* Gesenius on Isaiah.

† Before the time of Moses, that part of Moab which
lay north of the Arnon, had been conquered by the Amo-
rites, from whom it was afterward taken by the Israel-

of Rabbat Moab." This city, which was the capital of Moab, was called Rabbath-moab, to distinguish it from the Ammonite city of the same name; it is sometimes also called Ar; the Greeks called it Areopolis. The ruins which still bear the name of Rabba are situated about twenty-five miles south of the Arnon, on a low hill which commands the whole plain; those which now appear are comprehended within the circuit of a little more than a mile. There are several remains of private buildings, but none entire; and the only conspicuous objects among the ruins are the remains of a temple or palace, of which the walls and several niches are still standing, the gate of another building, two Corinthian columns, and an insulated altar in the plain: no traces of its walls are now to be found. Jerome says the city was overthrown by an earthquake when he was a young man.— The name of Dibon is still preserved in a ruined town called *Diban*, situated in a fine

ites, and given to the tribe of Reuben. When the tribes beyond Jordan were carried into captivity, the Moabites recovered this part of their old territory: they held it in the time of Isaiah and Jeremiah, and most of the cities of Moab mentioned by these prophets once belonged to the Israelites.

plain, about three miles north of the Arnon. The ruins, which are of considerable extent, present nothing of interest.——Heshbon, now called *Hesban,* was situated about sixteen miles north of the Arnon.   The ruins of a considerable town still exist, and cover the sides of an insulated hill.   There are a number of deep wells cut in the rocks, and also a large reservoir intended to hold water for the summer supply of the inhabitants.——The name of Medeba is still preserved in that of *Madeba,* applied to a large ruined town situated on a round hill about six miles south-east of Heshbon.   Here is an immense, well-built tank or cistern, one hundred and thirty yards wide by one hundred and fifteen deep, which, as there is no stream at Medeba, might still be of use to the Bedouins, were the surrounding ground cleared of the rubbish to allow the water to flow into it; but, as Burckhardt remarks, such an undertaking is far beyond the views of the wandering Arabs. Not a single edifice is standing; but on the west side of the town are the remains of a temple, built of large blocks of stone, and apparently of great antiquity.*—— Several other places might also be enumerated,

* Pictorial Bible—Seetzen—Burckhardt—Irby and Mangles—G. Robinson.

but as they "are remarkable for nothing but what is common to them with all the cities of Moab—their entire desolation"—it is needless to enter into further details.

Of all the cities in this region, Karrak, a frontier town on the southern border, is the only one now inhabited by man. In the early ages of Christianity it was an important city, and the seat of a bishopric; but "its walls have mostly fallen down, and Karrak can now justly lay claim to nothing more than the name of village."

"The spoiler hath come upon Moab,
And hath destroyed her strong holds;
Her cities are desolate, without any to dwell therein."

"In view of the prophecies and facts in relation to the land of Moab, we may observe, that we have here an evidence of the genuineness and truth of the sacred records. Here is a prophetic description of a land and its numerous towns, made nearly three thousand years ago, and in its minutest particulars it is sustained by all the travellers of modern times;—every successive visiter brings some additional confirmation of the truth of the prophecy.—The remains of once splendid cities, dilapidated walls, half demolished temples, and fragments broken and consumed by time, proclaim to the world that those cities are what the prophets, under the inspiration of God, foretold they would be."*

That such numerous cities, which had subsisted for so many ages, should, all of them, ever be reduced to such a state of utter desolation and desertion as that in which we now find them, was, in the time of the prophets, an event so utterly improbable as to surpass all human conception. They were then, and at a period long subsequent, in the most prosperous and flourishing condition. Their fate could only have been foreseen by HIM who knoweth the end from the beginning, and to whom the events of the future are as manifest as those that have long been past.

* Barnes on Isaiah.

CHAPTER VII.

PROPHECIES CONCERNING PHILISTIA.

The Philistines—Their origin and country—Prophecies concerning them—The Philistines as a people are extinct—Their country neglected and well nigh depopulated—Its present condition as described by Volney and Addison—Ancient Gaza destroyed and forsaken—Description of modern Gaza—Askelon desolate and uninhabited—Description of its ruins—Description of the valley between Askelon and Gaza—Former strength and importance, and present state of Ashdod—Ekron is utterly destroyed.

THE Philistines were descended from Mizraim, the second son of Ham, by whom Egypt was originally peopled. They seem to have left that country at an early period, and to have fixed themselves on the western coast of Canaan, expelling the Avites, by whom it had been previously occupied. The period of their settling in Canaan is unknown, but it must have been considerably before the time of Abraham. They soon became so powerful as to give to the whole country the name of PALESTINE, by which it was known even in the time of Moses, (Exod. xv, 14,) and under which it is mentioned by Greek and Roman writers. The part of Palestine actually occupied by the Philistines was, however, of very inconsiderable extent, being merely a narrow strip extending about sixty miles along the coast from the "river of Egypt," nearly to the bay of Joppa. This tract of country, which, as travellers inform us, is still called *Phalastin* by the natives, is naturally very fertile : on the distribution of the land of Canaan among the Israelites it fell to the lot of Judah, but the people of that tribe were never able to dispossess the Philistines of it. In the time of Joshua, the country of the Philistines was divided into five principalities or lordships ; namely, Gaza, Askelon, Ashdod, Gath and Ekron.

The following are some of the principal prophecies concerning this people, and their country :—

"Thus saith the Lord God ;
  'Behold, I will stretch out my hand upon the Philistines,
  And destroy the remnant of the sea-coasts.'"
EZEK. xxv, 16.

"Baldness is come upon Gaza ;*
Askelon is cut off with the remnant of their valley."
JER. xlvii, 5.

* Shaving the head was anciently, in Eastern countries, a token of mourning, and was commonly practised on occasion of the death of a relative, or in a time of general calamity. Isa. xxii, 12 ; Jer. xvi, 6 ; Micah i, 16. In allusion to this custom, the prophets use the term "baldness" in a figurative sense, to denote the misery that would follow the infliction of God's judgments upon guilty cities and nations. Thus in the present case, the expres-

" For three transgressions of Gaza, and for four,
I will not turn away the punishment thereof.
I will send a fire upon the walls of Gaza which shall
devour the palaces thereof.
And I will cut off the inhabitant from Ashdod,
And him that holdeth the sceptre from Askelon ;
And I will turn my hand against Ekron ;
And the remnant of the Philistines shall perish."
Amos i, 6–8.

' The king shall perish from Gaza,
And Askelon shall not be inhabited."   Zech. ix, 5.
" For Gaza shall be forsaken,
And Askelon a desolation :
They shall drive out Ashdod at the noon-day,
And Ekron shall be rooted up.
Wo unto the inhabitants of the sea-coasts,
The nation of the Cherethites !*
The word of the Lord is against you ;
O Canaan, the land of the Philistines,
I will even destroy thee that there shall be no inhabitant.
And the sea-coast shall be dwellings and cottages for
·shepherds, and folds for flocks."   Zech. ii, 4–6.

" *The remnant of the Philistines shall perish.*"
—The Philistines were the most powerful and
lasting enemies that the Israelites had to en-

sion " *baldness* shall come upon Gaza," signifies no more
than that it should be visited by some heavy calamity ;
and in this sense the word is used in several other prophecies. See Isa. xv, 2 ; Ezek. vii, 18 ; Amos viii, 10.

* The Cherethites were Philistines, as were also the
Pelethites.

counter. The history of the wars between the two people fills a large space in the historical books of Scripture, and these contests continued to be waged from the commencement of the Jewish commonwealth to its dissolution at the captivity. After the return of the Jews to their own country, the wars between the two nations were revived; but in the time of the Maccabees, the Philistines were completely subdued by the Jews, who took possession of the whole country. After this the Philistines did not long remain as a separate people; they probably became incorporated with the Jews who settled in their country, and hence, though they are before us from the commencement to the close of the Old Testament history, they are not once mentioned in the New Testament.

" *I will destroy the land of the Philistines that there shall be no inhabitant; and the sea-coast shall be dwellings and cottages for shepherds, and folds for flocks.*"—When this prophecy was delivered, and for many ages after, the land of the Philistines was a rich and well-cultivated region, with a numerous population, and strongly fortified cities. There could at that time have been no human probability of its eventual desolation; yet the words of the prophecy contain an accurate description of the state of that country at the present day, and for several centuries past. It partakes of the general desolation of Judea and the neighbouring states. Mr. Addison says,—" We were now in the country anciently inhabited by the warlike Philistines, the uncircumcised generation who at different times smote the Hebrews with great slaughter, and, in the memorable battle in which the ark of God was taken, ' slew of the Israelites thirty thousand footmen.' We were traversing the land renowned for the wonderful exploits of Samson. The country is vastly different from what it was in those times. The vineyards of Timnath no longer exist; nor are lions now anywhere to be found. At the present day, ' three hundred foxes turned tail to tail,' with ' a firebrand in the midst between two tails,' might range throughout the land without doing much damage, there being no longer ' the shocks and the standing corn, with the vineyards and olives,' to be burned up with fire, as at the period when Samson revenged himself on the Philistines for the loss of his wife.

By the expression, " it shall be without an inhabitant," we are to understand that the country should be in a great measure depopulated;

not that it should be literally without a single inhabitant. That this is the meaning of the prophet is evident from the words which immediately follow, and in which he describes the kind of persons by whom the country should be occupied. "And the sea-coast shall be dwellings and cottages for shepherds, and folds for flocks." And this, Mr. Richardson says, is the literal truth at present with respect to the Philistine coast in general, and in particular of Askelon and its vicinity.

But the most striking corroboration of the divine prediction is that supplied by Volney, in the account which he gives of the modern state of the land of the Philistines. "In the plain between Ramla and Gaza, we meet with a number of villages, badly built, of dried mud, and which, like the inhabitants, exhibit every mark of poverty and wretchedness. The houses, on a nearer view, are only so many huts, sometimes detached, and sometimes ranged in the form of cells around a court-yard, enclosed by a mud wall. In winter, the people and their cattle may be said to live together, the part of the dwelling allotted to themselves being only raised two feet above that in which they lodge their beasts.—The environs of these villages are sown, at the proper season, with grain and water-melons; all the rest is a desert, and abandoned to the Bedouin Arabs who feed their flocks on it. At every step we meet with ruins of towns, dungeons, and castles with fosses, and sometimes a garrison, consisting of the lieutenant of an Aga, and two or three Barbary soldiers, with nothing but a shirt and a musket; but more frequently they are inhabited by jackals, owls, and scorpions."

"*I will send a fire upon the walls of Gaza, which shall devour the palaces thereof—The king shall perish from Gaza.—Gaza shall be forsaken.*"—Gaza was situated on the Mediterranean coast, about sixty miles south-west of Jerusalem, and was the most southern of the Philistine principalities. Its situation as a frontier defence against Egypt, rendered it at all times a place of importance, and exposed it to many revolutions. In the year three hundred and thirty-one before Christ, it was taken, but not destroyed, by Alexander the Great, after the siege of Tyre; in one hundred and ninety-eight before Christ, it was taken and plundered by Antiochus, king of Syria; and one hundred years later, it was utterly destroyed by Alexander Janneus, king of Judea. It lay desolate about forty years, when it was rebuilt by

Gabinus, the Roman governor of Syria. It was afterward, according to Josephus, again destroyed by the Jews, with several other towns, to avenge a massacre of their country-men at Cesarea. This explains the expression used by St. Luke, who, in mentioning Gaza, observes that it was then " desert." Acts viii, 26.

Thus it appears that the Gaza which existed in the time of the prophets did actually become ruined and desolate. It was also literally " forsaken," as the modern town, though it retains the name, does not occupy the site of the old city, having been built nearer the sea. As modern Gaza is the only place of any note now existing in the country formerly occupied by the Philistines, some account of it, though not exactly illustrating the prophecy, may not be altogether out of place. The best description is that of Sandys, of which the following abridgment comprises the substance :—

" It stands upon a hill surrounded with valleys, and those again well-nigh environed with hills, most of them planted with all sorts of delicate fruits. The buildings mean, both of forme and matter ; the best but low, of rough stone, arched within, and flat on the top, including a quad-rangle ; the walls surmounting their roofes, wrought through with potsheards to catch and strike downe the refreshing winds, having spouts of the same, in colour, shape, and sight, resembling great ordnance. Others covered with mats and hurdles ; some built of mud ; amongst all, not any comely or convenient. Yet there are some reliques left, and some impressions, that testifie a better condition; for divers simple roofes are supported with goodly pillars of Parian marble, some plaine, some curiously carved A number broken in pieces doe serve for thresholds, jambs of doores, and sides of windowes. On the north-east corner and summitie of the hill are the ruines of huge arches, sunke low in the earth, and other foundations of a stately building.—On the west side of the city, out of sight, and yet within hearing, is the sea, seven furlongs off,* where they have a decayed and unsafe port, of small auaile at this day to the inhabitants. In the valley, on the east side of the city, are many straggling buildings."

" This is a more complete account of Gaza than any which later travellers give ; and the most of it is still applicable, except that some of the ancient remains of columns, &c., have disappeared. The town being surrounded by, and interspersed with, gardens and plantations

* Recent travellers make it more.

of olive and date trees, has a picturesque appearance; and the interior, though mean, disappoints expectation rather less than do most Syrian towns."—*Pict. Bible.*

"*Askelon shall be a desolation.—Askelon shall not be inhabited.*"—Askelon was situated about twelve miles north of Gaza, and was accounted the most strongly fortified town on the Philistine coast. It was seated on a hill which presents an abrupt, wave-beaten face to the sea, but slopes gently landward, where a ridge of rock winds around the town in a semicircular direction, terminating at each extremity in the sea. On this rock the walls were built, the foundations of which remain all the way around, and though generally ruined, maintain in some places their original elevation, which was considerable; they are of great thickness, and flanked with towers at different distances. It is remarkable that the ground falls within the walls, as it does on the outside; the town is, therefore, situated in a hollow, so that no part of the buildings could be seen from without the walls.

In the early ages of Christianity, Askelon became the seat of a bishopric; and in the time of the crusades, the degree of consequence which it still retained, and the strength of its position, caused its possession to be warmly contested between the Christians and the Saracens. Since the expulsion of the Christians it has ceased to be a place of any importance. " Sandys, early in the seventeenth century, describes it then as ' a place of no note ; more than that, the Turke doth keepe there a garrison.' It is now of still less note, being an entirely deserted ruin,—' a scene of desolation,' says Mr. Joliffe, 'the most complete I ever witnessed, except at Nicopolis.' "—*Pict. Bible.*

The fullest description of the present state of Askelon is that given by Mr. Addison, which, though too lengthy to be inserted entire, is yet too interesting to be altogether omitted. The following abridgment embraces the most important particulars :—" We now crossed a bare, uncultivated country, and the guide, pointing to a hill in front, upon which some crumbling walls were visible, announced to us ' the ruins of Askelon.' We ascended to the summit of the eminence, and clambering through a gap in the walls, over loose masses of stone, imbedded in cement, we gazed over a hollow valley, within which lay extended the solitary ruins of the once populous and flourishing city. On an eminence above towered the tottering walls of a ruined monastery, and around, in every direction, extended a succession of bare, arid sand-hills, bordered by a low and desolate sandy coast.

" Descending into the hollow, we wandered amid masses of masonry, heaps of stone, and mounds of rubbish.   Here and there we perceived the mutilated shafts of gray granite columns, and some broken pillars of coarse marble.   The foundations of walls and the ruins of houses encumbered the ground at every step, and the remains of gardens and of courts, once attached to the domestic habitations of the city, were plainly distinguishable on all sides.   These confused heaps present a scene of thorough desolation ; not a single column is erect, nor a single shaft entire.

" We wandered down to the sea-shore, and crossed over the shattered masses of wall which once formed the defences of the town toward the sea.   Askelon was the principal maritime town of the Philistines ; now not the vestige of a port is traceable.   A wild, solitary, naked coast stretches far away on either side, and no safe refuge for ships is now anywhere to be distinguished.

" The ruined monastery before alluded to was the last inhabited dwelling on the spot.   A few monks here sheltered themselves amid the ruins of the once populous city, and for a long time struggled against the genius of desolation which brooded over the place; they cultivated a little garden, and subsisted on the charity of distant brethren. Their resources, however, at last diminished—the support from abroad was withdrawn—the building was gradually allowed to go to ruin; some of the monks sought refuge in other establishments, and the last of the inhabitants of Askelon was laid in his sandy grave many a year back. Upon this forlorn spot, where once was congregated a large population, and where once stood the proudest of the five satrapies of the Philistines, there is now not a single inhabitant. There is not a dwelling near the place, and the surrounding country is deserted and uncultivated. Askelon is become ' a desolation,' it is ' not inhabited.' "

"Baldness is come upon Gaza; Askelon is cut off with the remnant of their valley."—The prophet in this passage evidently alludes to the valley lying between Gaza and Askelon. Sandys gives an interesting description of the natural beauty and fertility, and at the same time neglected and desolate condition of this

tract of country. He says,—"Wee past this day through the most pregnant and pleasant valley that ever eye beheld. On the right hand a ridge of high mountaines, whereon stands Hebron; on the left hand the Mediterranean Sea, bordered with continuous hills, beset with varietie of fruits; as they are for the most part of this daye's iourney. The champaine betweene, about twentie miles over full of flowry hils ascending leasurely, and not much surmounting their ranker valleys, with groves of olives and other fruits dispersedly adorned. Yet is this wealthy bottome (as are all the rest) for the most part uninhabited but only for a few small and contemptible villages, possessed by barbarous Moores, [Arabs,] who till no more than will serve to feed them :—the grasse waste-high, unmowed, uneaten, and uselessly withering."

" *I will cut off the inhabitants from Ashdod.—Ashdod shall be driven out at noon-day.*"—This town was situated between Ekron on the north and Askelon on the south. It was nearer to the sea than the former, but not so near as the latter, which seems to have been the only one of the five that stood close out to the shore. It was anciently a place of much importance, and was surrounded by a wall of great strength. It is distinguished for having sustained the longest siege recorded in history, having been besieged for twenty-nine years by Psammitticus, king of Egypt. In the time of the Maccabees, it was taken and destroyed by the Jews. It was probably to this event that the preceding prophecies referred. Under the Romans, Ashdod was rebuilt, and it is mentioned in Acts viii, 40, under the name of Azotus. In the early ages of Christianity it became the seat of a bishopric, and it continued to be a fair village till the time of Jerome. It is now an inconsiderable place. Volney says,— " Leaving Yabna, we met successively with various ruins, the most considerable of which are at *Ezdoud*, the ancient Azotus, famous at present for its scorpions. This town, so powerful under the Philistines, affords no proof of its ancient importance."

"I will turn my hand against Ekron.—Ekron shall be rooted up."—This was the most northern of the Philistine cities. " In the time of Jerome it was a large village, and was then called *Accaron*. In the time of Breidenbachius, whose Travels were first published in 1486, it had declined from a village to a solitary cot-

15

tage or hut, which still bore the ancient name. No traces of the name or site can now be discovered."—*Pict. Bible.* Dr. Robinson found, near the spot where Ekron must have been situated, a village named Akir, which, he says, "there seems no reason to doubt, answers to the ancient Ekron. It is of considerable size; but we could perceive nothing to distinguish it from other modern villages of the plain. Like them it is built of unburnt bricks or mud; and exhibits to the eye of the traveller no marks of antiquity." Whether this village occupies the site of the ancient city of the Philistines or not, the integrity of the prophecy is not in any way affected by it, Akir being only a *modern village*, exhibiting *no marks of antiquity*. The Ekron of Scripture *is* "rooted up:" so completely has the prediction been accomplished, that not a ruin is left to designate the spot on which the city stood.

Thus have the prophecies respecting Philistia been accomplished: the people have perished, and the land is mostly desolate; ancient Gaza has been demolished and forsaken; Askelon is a desolation, and its ruins do not shelter a single inhabitant; the inhabitants are cut off from Ashdod; and Ekron is rooted up.

CHAPTER VIII.

PROPHECIES CONCERNING NINEVEH.

Obscurity of its early history—Its situation, and antiquity—
Its extraordinary dimensions—Diodorus's account of it—Was not
a compactly built city—Probable number of inhabitants—Nineveh
a commercial city—Was an exceedingly wicked as well as great
city—Jonah's mission—Repentance of the Ninevites—Their
relapse—Nahum foretels the fall of Nineveh—Remarks on Nahum's prophecies—Substance of his predictions—Zephaniah's
prophecy respecting Nineveh—Prosperous state of Nineveh
when these prophecies were uttered—Nineveh taken by the
Medes and Babylonians—Particulars of its siege and capture,
showing the literal fulfilments of the prophecies—The final and
utter desolation of Nineveh foretold—Accomplishment of this
prediction—Notices respecting the site of Nineveh, from several
modern travellers—Conclusion.

"Of the early history of the great Assyrian
empire, little is with certainty known. The
bewildering antiquity of its origin—the im-
mensity of its dominion—the splendour and
gigantic bulk of its cities—and the utter desolation that, for long ages, has overspread them,
invest the subject with the character of a magnificent dream. Yet that such cities as Nineveh and Babylon have existed, and with a
grandeur perhaps never since equalled, we cannot but believe. The ashes still remain to
prove that the Titanic forms have been;" and
their extent and splendour are recorded on the
page of both sacred and profane history.

"There are few ruins of ancient cities around which lingers a stronger interest than those of Nineveh. It was one of the first founded cities in the world. Its reputed greatness has almost the air of an eastern fable. It was the theatre of an extraordinary mission of one Hebrew prophet, while another foretold its desolation in words of brief but terrible import."*

Nineveh was the capital of the first Assyrian empire, and stood on the bank of the river Tigris. There is some uncertainty as to its exact site, but the testimony of most ancient writers concurs with the local traditions to fix it on the eastern bank of the river, opposite the modern town of Mosul, where there are several extensive mounds of decayed ruins, and where the little village of Nunia [Nineveh] still preserves the remembrance of its name. It was one of the most ancient cities of the world, having been founded shortly after the deluge, by Asshur the son of Shem,† Gen. x, 11, but it did not rise to any considerable greatness until many centuries after, when, about the year 1230 B. C. it was enlarged by

* American Biblical Repository, vol. ix.

† From him also the country derived its name ; *Asshur* being the Hebrew word for Assyria,

Ninus, its second founder, and became the greatest city in the world, and mistress of the East.

In Jonah iii, 3, it is said that "Nineveh was an exceeding great city of three days' journey;" that is, the circuit, or *circumference*, of the city was three days' journey: and with this agree the accounts of ancient writers, who estimate the circuit of Nineveh at four hundred and eighty stadia,* which will make three days' journey, one hundred and fifty stadia being, according to Herodotus, the common computation of a day's journey for a foot traveller. In form, the city was not square, but oblong; its greatest length extended along the bank of the Tigris, while its breadth reached from the river to the eastern hills.

As none of the ancient historians who mention Nineveh lived till after its destruction, their accounts, derived from old records and reports, are necessarily brief and imperfect. The best account is that given by Diodorus, who states, that Ninus, one of the kings of Assyria, having surpassed all his predecessors in

* If Roman stadia are here meant, it would make the circumference of Nineveh to be sixty miles; but if, as is more probable, Greek stadia are intended, then it would be only forty-eight miles; the Roman stadium being one-eighth, and the Greek one-tenth of a mile.

the glory and success of his arms, resolved to build a city of such state and grandeur, that it should not only be the greatest then in the world, but such as no king after him should easily be able to exceed. Accordingly, having brought a vast number of his forces together, and provided every thing which his design required, he built near the Tigris a city very famous for its walls and fortifications. Its length was one hundred and fifty stadia, its breadth ninety, and its circumference four hundred and eighty.* It was surrounded by a wall one hundred feet high, and so thick that three chariots could easily be driven upon it abreast; and the wall was fortified and adorned with fifteen hundred towers, each of which was two hundred feet high. Diodorus adds, that the founder was not deceived in his expectations, for no one ever after built a city equal to it in the extent of its circumference, and the magnificence of its walls.†

* This statement of the form and dimensions of ancient Nineveh corresponds with the local features of its supposed site; for though it might have stretched its front along the river to any extent, yet its breadth was limited to about ten miles, that being the width of the plain between the river and the range of hills which formed the eastern boundary of the city.

† Pictorial Bible.

We must not, however, suppose that the whole of the vast enclosure of Nineveh was covered with compact streets and buildings; it doubtless, like ancient Babylon, and like many large Oriental cities of the present day, contained extensive plantations and gardens, as well as pastures for the "much cattle" that were in the city. Jonah iv, 11. "The extent of Eastern cities, therefore, forms but little guide in estimating the number of their inhabitants. The compact, close streets of our cities, present a striking contrast to the scattered mansions of the East, surrounded with their extensive courts and gardens, occupying at least an even portion of the whole area. An equal space, therefore, was far from containing an equal number of men as with us."*

Of the population of Nineveh we have no account, except the statement in Jonah iv, 11, that it contained "more than sixscore thousand persons that could not discern their right hand from their left." By this form of expression, young children are commonly understood, and as these are generally reckoned to form one-fifth of the inhabitants of any place, the population of Nineveh may be estimated to have been upward of six hundred thousand

* Heeren's Historical Researches.

persons. This calculation exhibits the force of the remarks made in the preceding paragraph; for the city of London, which does not occupy more than one-fourth of the ground which Nineveh did, contains a population of two millions.

Nineveh was situated very commodiously for the purposes of commerce. The river Tigris opened a ready communication with the Persian Gulf, Southern Asia, and the shores of the Indian Ocean. Of these advantages the Ninevites seem to have duly availed themselves, for they are said by Nahum to have " multiplied their merchants as the stars of heaven," Nahum iii, 16.

But as in other great and rich cities, so in Nineveh, there prevailed extreme depravity of morals. So great was the wickedness of its inhabitants, that Jehovah commissioned the prophet Jonah to " go to Nineveh and cry against it," Jonah i, 2. The word of the Lord came unto him, saying, " Arise, go up to Nineveh, that great city, and preach unto it the preaching that I bid thee." So Jonah arose, and went to Nineveh, and proclaimed through the streets of the city, " Yet forty days and Nineveh shall general repentance and humiliation of the people. The king, as soon as he heard the message of the prophet, arose from his throne, laid aside his robes, and covered himself with sackcloth. He also proclaimed a fast; and the people put on sackcloth, and cried mightily to God, and turned from their evil ways; for they said, "Who can tell if God will turn away from his fierce anger, that we perish not?" "And God saw their works, that they turned from their evil way; and God repented of the evil that he had said he would do unto them; and he did it not," Jonah iii, 5–10.

The repentance of the Ninevites appears, however, to have been more deep than lasting. Their sudden reformation proved to be of no long continuance; "like the morning cloud, and the early dew," it soon passed away, and they turned again to their folly, increasing in wickedness until their iniquities again aroused the righteous anger of an offended God. Accordingly, some years after, we find the prophet Nahum foretelling the final and utter destruction of Nineveh; indeed, his whole prophecy relates to the overthrow of that city and the proud empire of which it was capital.

Speaking of Nahum, Bishop Lowth remarks, —"None of the minor prophets are equal to

him in boldness, ardour, and sublimity. His
prophecy forms a regular and perfect poem;
the exordium is not merely magnificent, it is
truly majestic; the preparation for the destruction of Nineveh, and the description of its
downfall and desolation, are expressed in the
most vivid colours, and are bold and luminous
in the highest degree."*   Dr. A. Clarke observes, that his description is "so lively and
pathetic, that he seems to have been upon the
spot to declare to the Ninevites the ruin of their
city."   The following passages embrace the
substance of his predictions :—

"THE BURDEN OF NINEVEH.

" God is jealous, and the Lord revengeth;
The Lord revengeth, and is furious;
The Lord will take vengeance on his adversaries;
And he reserveth wrath for his enemies.
The Lord is slow to anger, and great in power,
And will not at all acquit the wicked:
The Lord hath his way in the whirlwind and the storm,
And the clouds are the dust of his feet.
Who can stand before his indignation?
And who can abide the fierceness of his anger?
    " The Lord is good, a strong hold in the day of trouble;
And he knoweth them that trust in him.
But with an overrunning flood
He will make an utter end of the place thereof,

* Lectures on Hebrew Poetry.

And darkness shall pursue his enemies.
What do ye imagine against the Lord?
He will make an utter end:
Affliction shall not rise up the second time.
For while they be folden together as thorns,
And while they are drunken as drunkards,
They shall be devoured as stubble fully dry."

CHAP. i, 1–3, 6–10.

" The gates of the river shall be opened,
And the palace shall be dissolved.
Take ye the spoil of silver, take the spoil of gold;
For there is none end of the store and glory
Out of all the pleasant furniture.
She is empty, void, and waste;
And the heart melteth, and the knees smite together."

CHAP. ii, 6, 9, 10.

' Wo to the bloody city!
It is all full of lies and robbery.
Behold, I am against thee, saith the Lord of hosts;
And I will show the nations thy nakedness,
And the kingdoms thy shame.
And it shall come to pass
That all they that look upon thee shall flee from thee,
And say, ' Nineveh is laid waste.' "—CHAP. iii, 1, 5, 6.

These predictions were delivered soon after the carrying away of the ten tribes by the Assyrians, and about the time of Sennacherib's invasion of Judah, in the reign of Hezekiah. At a subsequent period, during the reign of Josiah, the fall of Nineveh was foretold by the prophet Zephaniah, in the following words :—

" The Lord will stretch out his hand against the north,
And destroy Assyria;
And will make Nineveh a desolation,
And dry like a wilderness.
And flocks shall lie down in the midst of her,
All the beasts of the nations.
This is the rejoicing city that dwelt carelessly,
That said in her heart, ' I am, and there is none beside
   me.'
How is she become a desolation,
A place for beasts to lie down in!
Every one that passeth by her shall hiss and wag his
   hand."   ZEPH. ii, 13–15.

When these prophets predicted the desolation of Nineveh, that city was in the height of its glory, and its king the mightiest monarch of his day;

" For all the East was his,
From Indus westward to the Hellespont,—
From north of Caspian to the Persian Gulf,
A host of nations, whom no tongue could sum,
All called Assyria lord; and year by year,
To giant Nineveh new warriors sent
To guard her monarch's state, and grace his throne."
              ATHERSTONE'S *Fall of Nineveh.*

The destruction of Nineveh was accomplished by the confederate forces of the Medes and Babylonians; but there is considerable discrepancy in the accounts of ancient writers, as to the time when, and the principal agents by whom it was effected. "In the *circumstances* of the great event, however, these writers substantially agree with one another, and with the inspired writers; and as the circumstances alone are mentioned by the latter, and as circumstantial corroborations are of the most interest and importance, we shall confine our notices to them. We shall follow the account of Diodorus, which is not only the most complete and connected which remains to us, but is proved to be generally accurate by the remarkable illustration which it affords to, and receives from, the prophecies of Scripture "*

It was foretold by the prophet, that a great destruction should befall the Assyrians while they were in a state of drunkenness. "*While they are drunken as drunkards, they shall be devoured as stubble fully dry.*"—On the advance of the allied forces of the Medes and Babylonians, the king of Assyria marched against them, and defeated them in three successive battles. Elated with these victories, the Assyrians abandoned themselves to revelry and feasting. The invaders, "being informed, by some deserters, of the negligence and drunkenness in the enemy's camp, assaulted them un-

* Pictorial Bible.

expectedly by night, and falling orderly on them disorderly, and prepared on them unprepared, easily made themselves masters of the camp, slew many of the soldiers, and drove the rest into the city."

"*Thy shepherds slumber, O king of Assyria,*" Nahum iii, 18.—These words plainly intimate that the Assyrians should, in the day of their calamity, be deserted by those upon whom they relied for assistance. And such was the fact. The Assyrians despatched messengers to the various tributary provinces, calling upon them for succour ; but they, instead of rendering any aid, either continued in a state of inactivity, or went over to the enemy. Even the Bactrians, who had actually marched with a large army to their assistance, before they reached Nineveh, were induced to renounce their allegiance and join the invaders.

The Assyrians being now shut up within the walls of the city, took the most active measures for their defence. The city was well stored with provisions, and the strong and lofty walls seemed to defy any force which the besiegers could bring against them. Such were the strength and resources of the place, that nothing of any consequence was effected by the besiegers for two years. But the end came at last, and in the manner which the prophet had foretold.

"*With an overrunning flood will he make an utter end of the place thereof.—The gates of the river shall be opened.*"—These passages clearly indicate the agency of an inundation in effecting the overthrow of the city. And this, according to Diodorus, was the case. He says, —"There was an old tradition, that Nineveh could not be taken unless the river first became an enemy to the city. In the third year of the siege, the river, being swollen by continual rains, overflowed part of the city, and threw down twenty stadia of the wall. The king, then imagining that the oracle was accomplished, and that the river was now manifestly become an enemy to the city, cast aside all hope of safety; and to avoid falling into the hands of the enemy, he built a large funeral pile in the palace, and having collected his gold and silver, and royal vestments, together with all his household, placed himself with them in an apartment built in the midst of the pile, and burned them, himself, and the palace together. When the besiegers heard of the death of the king, they entered in by the breach which the waters had made, and took the city." Thus was the prophecy of Nahum literally fulfilled ; *the gates of the river were opened, and the palace was dissolved,* or burned. It is worthy of remark, that the agency of *fire,* as well as water, in the destruction of Nineveh, was also foretold by the prophet. Nahum iii, 13, 15.

It was predicted that the besiegers would find much spoil when they took the city.— " *Take ye the spoil of silver, and the spoil of gold; for there is none end of the store,*" &c.—Accordingly Diodorus describes the conquerors of Nineveh as being greatly enriched by the booty which they found there ; many talents of gold and silver* were collected from the ashes of the funeral pile, and the rubbish of the burned palace of the Assyrian king.

The entire destruction, and perpetual desolation of Nineveh, were also foretold.—" *The Lord will make Nineveh a desolation, a place for beasts to lie down in.—He will make an utter end : affliction shall not rise up a second time.*"—Nineveh, after its capture, went rapidly to ruin, and its decay was doubtless hastened by the enlargement and beautifying of Babylon, and the

* A talent of silver is worth about $1,700, a talent of gold about $27,000.

removal of the seat of empire to that city. The most ancient of the Greek writers who mention Nineveh, speak of it as a place that had long been desolate. Lucian, who lived and wrote in the second century after Christ, says,— " Nineveh is so utterly destroyed, that no vestige of it remains, nor is it easy to tell the spot where it formerly stood. In the year 637, the emperor Heraclius defeated the Persians in a great action fought on the convenient battle-field offered by the vacant site of Nineveh."* Haitho, the Armenian, in 1300, says,—" This city is totally ruined." " Master John Cartwright," who was there in the latter part of the sixteenth century, after giving a summary of the ancient accounts of the great Nineveh, adds,—" Now it is destroyed, as God foretold it should bee by the Chaldeans, being nothing else than a sepulchre of herselfe." In a later age (1657) Thevenot remarks,—" This city stood on the east side of the river, where-are to be seen some of its ruins of great extent even to this day." Tavernier states, that " the ancient city of Nineveh is now a heap of rubbish only, for a league along the river, full of vaults and caverns."

Niebuhr has the following remarks,—" As

* Gibbon, chap. 6.

one comes to Mosul, in this direction, he will pass through Nineveh. I was not aware that I was passing over so remarkable a spot, till I was near the river. Here they pointed out to me a village on a large hill, which was called Nunia, and a mosque in which (it is said) the prophet Jonah lies buried. Another hill on this ground was called *Kalla Nunia*, or the ' Castle of Nineveh.'—While I was at Mosul, the walls of Nineveh were pointed out to me. These I had not before observed in my tour thither, but took them for a part of the hill."

All that is now to be seen in this spot are numerous mounds,* supposed to consist of ruins, but which are covered with earth, and grown over with grass. " It is not easy," observes Mr. Rich, " to say precisely what are ruins and what are not; what is art converted by the

---

* Mr. Buckingham observes, that " these mounds and smaller heaps of ruins are scattered widely over the plain, sufficient to prove that the site of the original city occupied a vast extent, notwithstanding that some of the latest visiters to this place have thought that the remains were confined to the few mounds in the centre only." He also remarks, that the distance to which the mounds extend, left no doubt in his mind that the dimensions of Nineveh were fully equal to the accounts given of it by ancient geographers and historians

lapse of ages into the semblance of nature, and what is merely nature broken by the hand of time in the ruins approaching in their appearance to those of art."*　Such an "utter end" has been made of Nineveh, that even its very ruins may be said to have been long ago ruined and destroyed.

> "Fallen is the mighty city! fallen, fallen!
> Fallen is great Nineveh,—the city of old,—
> The mighty city, queen of all the earth!
> The day of her exulting is gone by!
> Her throne is in the dust! her sceptre broke!
> Her walls are gone! her palaces dissolved!
> The desert is around her, and within.—
> Like shadows has the mighty passed away!
> And scarce remains a solitary stone
> To say, 'Here stood imperial Nineveh?'"
>
> ATHERSTONE.

Her "nobles dwell in the dust," and the busy crowds who once thronged her streets are nowhere to be found.　Her magnificent walls, her lofty towers, her gorgeous temples, and her splendid palaces, which, from the massiveness of their structure, seemed to claim com-

* "From some of these mounds, large stones, frequently with bitumen adhering to them, are dug out.　In general, I think there were but very few bricks used in the building of Nineveh."—*Rich.*　The ruins of Babylon, on the contrary, are composed entirely of bricks.

panionship with eternity, have passed away, leaving so little trace of their existence, that on the spot where they once stood,

> " The distant traveller, wearied with long search,
>   Leans on his staff, and wonders where had been
>   The city of old Ninus."

" This is the rejoicing city that dwelt carelessly, that said in her heart, ' I am, and there is none beside me.' How is she become a desolation, a place for beasts to lie down in! Every one that passeth by her shall hiss, and wag his hand,' Zeph. ii, 15.

CHAPTER IX.

PROPHECIES CONCERNING BABYLON.

Antiquity of Babylon—Description of Babylonia—Its fertility—
Its natural advantages—Commerce of Babylon—Its manufactures—Early history—Prosperity under Nebuchadnezzar—Description of the ancient city—Palace, hanging-gardens, and
temple of Belus—Prophecies concerning it—It is besieged, as
was foretold, by Cyrus—His army composed of "many nations
from the north country"—The city is taken by stratagem during
the time of a feast—Various prophecies fulfilled in the circumstances of its capture—It is taken a second time, by Darius, who
breaks down its walls—Its temples plundered and demolished by
Xerxes—Alexander proposes to restore Babylon, but is cut off by
death—It becomes desolate and forsaken—Its walls are utterly
destroyed—Its ruins, deserted by man, are tenanted by wild
beasts—Its site uncultivated—The land of Chaldea now mostly
a barren waste—Babylon become "a desolation and an astonishment"—Description of its principal ruins—The Amram Hill—The
Kasr—The Mujelibe—The Birs Nimrood—Reflections.

AFTER the fall of Nineveh, Babylon succeeded to the empire of the East, and became the metropolis of the second Assyrian
kingdom.

In point of antiquity, Babylon was superior
to Nineveh. Its foundation must be carried
back to the period (supposed to have been
about two hundred years after the flood) when
the inhabitants of the earth, probably under the
conduct of Nimrod, (Gen. x, 10,) "journeyed
from the east to a plain in the land of Shinar,"

and there commenced the erection of the oldest
city of which history has preserved any record. Gen. xi, 4–9: "And they said, 'Go to,
let us build us a city, and a tower whose top
may reach unto heaven; and let us make us a
name, lest we be scattered abroad upon the
face of the whole earth.' And the Lord came
down to see the city and the tower, which the
children of men builded. And the Lord said,
'Behold, the people is one, and they have all
one language; and this they begin to do: and
now nothing will be restrained from them,
which they have imagined to do. Go to, let us
go down, and there confound their language,
that they may not understand one another's
speech.' So the Lord scattered them abroad
from thence upon the face of all the earth: and
they left off to build the city. Therefore is the
name of it called BABEL," which signifies "confusion;" and hence its future name, *Babel On,*
that is, "The city of Babel."

The land of Babylonia or Chaldea, of which
Babylon was the capital, was situated between
the Euphrates and the Tigris, the former
bounding it on the west, the latter on the east.
The country enclosed by these two rivers was
one vast, uninterrupted level, indebted to them

for its fertility.* It was everywhere intersected by canals of various sizes; some, running across the country from one river to the other, answered the double purpose of a communication between them, and of irrigating the soil; while others were formed solely for the latter object. On the banks of these canals were innumerable machines for raising the water, and spreading it over the soil. This constant irrigation was rendered necessary by the heat, and almost constant dryness of the climate, as it seldom rains in that country. The fertility of this region was almost without parallel. The labours of the husbandman were rewarded with such a luxuriant crop, that Herodotus, fearful of being suspected of exaggeration, hesitated to state the full truth. He says,—" Of all the countries that I have visited, this is by far the most fruitful in corn. The soil is so well adapted to its growth, that it commonly yields two hundred fold, and in seasons remarkably favourable it sometimes

---

* The importance of these rivers to the Babylonians, and the value of their waters in irrigating the land, is thus spoken of in Ezekiel xxxi, 4: "The waters made him great, the deep set him up on high with her rivers running round about his plants, and sent out her little rivers to all the trees of the field."

amounts to three hundred. The leaves both of the wheat and the barley in this region are four fingers broad. But the immense height to which the millet and sesame [Indian corn] stalks grow, although I have witnessed it myself, I dare not mention, lest those who have not travelled in this region should disbelieve my report." This fertility with respect to corn was however somewhat counterbalanced by a dearth of timber. The fig tree, the olive, and the vine were not found there at all; and the want of them was but indifferently supplied by an abundance of date or palm trees, with which Babylonia was completely covered, and which still grow in large quantities on the banks of the Euphrates. Of all other large trees Babylonia was entirely destitute.

Like most level countries, Babylonia was as destitute of stone as of wood. The want of these important building materials was, however, compensated by an inexhaustible supply of superior clay, which, when dried in the sun or burned in the fire, furnished bricks so durable, that the remains of ancient buildings, which have been thrown down for centuries, have withstood the effects of the atmosphere to the present day.

The natural advantages of this region, both

in a political and commercial point of view, were very great. A single glance at the map of Asia is sufficient to show that somewhere in the vicinity of Babylon is the natural seat of empire in the East ; and that few places were more eligibly situated for a vast trade, as it was conducted before the discovery of a passage to India by way of the Cape of Good Hope. Amid all the changes of the Eastern world, empire and commerce seem to have been ever disposed to take up their abode on the banks of the Tigris and Euphrates. Notwithstanding the numerous revolutions it underwent, and the devastations of the barbarous conquerors who invaded it, this region presented an astonishing succession of flourishing cities, which, like the phœnix, seemed to arise from the ashes and ruins of their own destruction. Thus in the earliest periods of history we find Nineveh on the Tigris, and Babylon on the Euphrates, mighty and magnificent commercial cities, and the proud capitals of vast empires. When these fell, Seleucia arose on the banks of the Tigris, as if prosperity and power were unwilling to forsake the fertile plains watered by these rivers. Ere Seleucia fell, it was eclipsed by Ctesiphon, the capital of the Parthian empire. When both these were destroyed by the conquering Saracens, the royal cities of Bagdad and Ormus arose in their place, and became like them the home of the learned and the resort of the merchant; and the last glimmer, as it were, of the ancient splendour of Babylon seems still to hover over the half-ruined Bussora.*

The fact that there was in this region such a succession of celebrated cities, demonstrates that it possessed some important commercial advantages. " Nature herself seems to have formed it for the great seat of the international commerce of Asia. Situated between the Indus and the Mediterranean, it was the natural staple of such precious wares of the East as were esteemed in the West. Its proximity to the Persian Gulf, the great highway of trade, which nature seems to have prepared for the admission of the sea-faring nations of the Indian seas into the midst of Asia, must be reckoned as another advantage, especially when taken in connection with its vicinity to the two great rivers, the continuation, as it were, of this highway, and opening a communication with the nations dwelling on the Euxine and Caspian Seas. Thus favoured by nature, this country necessarily became the

* Heeren's Researches—Barnes on Isaiah.

central point, where the merchants of nearly all the nations of the civilized world assembled; and such, we are informed by history, it remained, so long as the international commerce of Asia flourished. Neither the devastating sword of conquering nations, nor the heavy yoke of Asiatic despotism, could tarnish, though for a while they might dim its splendour. It was only when Europeans found a new path to India, across the ocean, and converted the great commerce of the world from a land trade to a sea trade, that the royal city on the banks of the Tigris and Euphrates began to decline."— *Heeren.*

From the foregoing particulars it will at once be seen that Babylon owed its greatness not less to its commercial advantages than to its conquests, and its being the capital of a vast empire. From both sacred and profane history we learn that it was early distinguished for its commerce and manufactures. In Ezekiel xvii, 4, it is called " a land of traffic,—a city of merchants." The merchandise of the East, we are told by Strabo and Herodotus, passed through Babylon, and thence to Asia Minor. The merchants of Babylon were in communication with the surrounding countries, partly by caravans over land, and partly by sea through the Persian Gulf. Their possession of a maritime commerce may be inferred from that passage in Isaiah (xliii, 14) where the Chaldeans are spoken of as a people "whose cry [or exultation] is in their ships." "The accounts of ancient writers also concur in representing Babylon as a city which received the merchandise of the south—Arabian and Indian productions—by means of the Persian Gulf."—*Heeren.* The principal articles which they imported from these countries were gold and silver, precious stones, pearls, dyes, cinnamon, and other spicery, wood for building ships, and cotton.

The productions of their own skill and industry also formed a considerable item in the commerce of the Babylonians. "Carpets, one of the principal articles of luxury in the East, were nowhere so finely woven, and in such splendid colours, as at Babylon. Foreign nations made use of these carpets in the decoration of their harems and royal saloons. Among the Persians, not only the floors, but even the beds and sofas in the houses of the nobles were covered with these carpets. Babylonish garments were not less esteemed. Josh. vii, 21. It appears that they were usually of cotton, and the most costly were so highly valued for their brilliancy of colour, and fineness of texture, as to be compared to those of Media, and set apart for royal use. The superiority of Babylonish robes and carpets will not be a matter of surprise, when we consider how near Babylon was to Caramania on the one side, and to Arabia and Syria on the other, and that in these countries the finest wool and cotton were produced."—*Heeren.*

The early history of Babylon is, like that of Nineveh, involved in considerable obscurity. In the accounts of its rise and growth, as given by heathen writers, the facts of its history are so mixed up with fabulous legends, that it is impossible to separate the one from the other; and the sacred writers, after giving an account of its origin, in Genesis x and xi, make no further mention of it until the time of Hezekiah, when, as we are informed in 2 Kings xx, 12, " Berodach-baladan, the son of Baladan, king of Babylon, sent letters and a present to Hezekiah: for he had heard that Hezekiah had been sick." Previous to this, Babylon, though a rich and powerful, was not an independent, city. Babylonia was a province of the great Assyrian empire, and the predecessors of Berodach-baladan were merely prefects or viceroys of the kings of Nineveh. But about this time, the governors of Babylon and Media, probably taking advantage of a reverse of fortune which had befallen Sennacherib, the Assyrian monarch, (2 Kings xix, 35, 36,) had asserted their independence, and were now in a state of rebellion. " Berodach had, therefore, the same political interests as Hezekiah, in opposition to the king of Assyria; and it is not improbable that the. embassy which he sent *professedly* to congratulate Hezekiah on his recovery from his sickness, had for its *real* object the bringing of the king of Judah into an alliance against the common enemy."*

The Babylonians were, however, again reduced to subjection by Esarhaddon, the son of Sennacherib; but they soon after revolted a second time, and with better success; for they not only succeeded in effecting their independence, but, from being the vassals, they soon became the rivals, and at length, in conjunction with the Medes, the destroyers of Nineveh.

The most brilliant epoch in the history of Babylon was the period during which Nebuchadnezzar filled the throne of the kingdom. This mighty monarch, having subdued nearly all the surrounding countries, turned his atten-

* Pictorial Bible.

tion to the aggrandizement of his metropolis, employing his vast resources in its extension and embellishment. It was during his long and prosperous reign, which lasted from the year 605 to 562 B. C., that Babylon acquired that extent and magnificence, and those stupendous works were completed, which rendered it the wonder and admiration of the ancient world. This we learn from Daniel iv, 30, and also from Berosus, a Chaldean historian, who, in a fragment of his works preserved by Josephus,* says,—"Nabuchodonosor adorned the temple of Belus, and the other temples, after an elegant manner, out of the spoils he had taken in war. He also rebuilt the old city, and added another to it on the outside, and so far restored Babylon, that none who should besiege it afterward might have it in their power to divert the river, so as to facilitate an entrance into it; and this he did by building three walls about the inner city, and three about the outer. Some of these walls he built of burned brick and bitumen, and some of brick only. So when he had thus fortified the city with walls, and had adorned the gates magnificently, he added a new palace to that which his father had dwelt in, and that more eminent in its height, and in

* Against Apion, book i, sec. 19.

its great splendour. Now in this palace he erected very high walks, supported by stone pillars, and by planting what was called a pensile paradise, and replenishing it with all sorts of trees, he rendered the prospect an exact resemblance of a mountainous country."

It would occupy too much room to insert at length the descriptions of Babylon given by ancient writers; we must therefore limit ourselves to the following brief particulars.

Babylon was built in the form of a square, having four equal sides of one hundred and twenty stadia, or twelve miles each. It stood on the banks of the Euphrates, which ran through its midst, dividing it into two parts, of which that on the western side was the older, but that on the eastern the more magnificent.

The city was surrounded by a wall forty-eight miles in circumference, and, according to Herodotus, eighty-seven feet in thickness, and three hundred and fifty high.[*] It was further defended by a wide and deep moat or ditch,

---

[*] The prophet Jeremiah, in the following passages, alludes to the extraordinary dimensions of the wall of Babylon:—" Though Babylon should *mount up to heaven*, and though she should fortify the *height* of her strength," &c. —" The *broad walls* of Babylon shall be utterly broken," Jer. li, 53, 58.

lined with brickwork, and filled with water, which went entirely around the city ; some idea of its capacity may be formed from the fact that the earth dug out of it furnished the bricks with which the wall was built. In the walls were one hundred gates, twenty-five on each side, which were all made of solid brass, and of prodigious size and strength. Between every two of these gates were three towers ten feet higher than the walls, and four more at the angles of the wall, and three more between each of these angles and the next gate on either side. These towers, however, were built only on three sides of the city, being omitted on one side where the morasses rendered the protection which they offered unnecessary. From the twenty-five gates on each side of the city, were twenty-five streets one hundred and fifty feet in width, extending in straight lines to the corresponding gates on the opposite side, and dividing the city into six hundred and seventy-six squares, each of which was nearly two miles in circumference. Round these squares, facing the streets, stood the houses, all of which were three or four stories high. The ground in the interior of the squares was not built upon, but laid out in fields, gardens, and pleasure grounds.

That part of the river which ran through the city was faced with brick, and on each of its banks was a brick wall corresponding in height with that on the outside of the city. In each of these walls were twenty-five brazen gates, from which were steps leading down from the streets to the river, for the convenience of the inhabitants who passed and repassed in boats from one side of the city to the other. These gates were always open during the day, but closed at night. The communication between the two divisions of the city was further assisted by a bridge, thirty feet in width, which crossed the river near the centre.

The most remarkable structures within the city were the palace, the hanging-gardens, and the temple.

The *palace*, built by Nebuchadnezzar, stood on the eastern side of the river. With its parks and gardens it occupied an area of four and a half square miles, which was enclosed by a triple wall. Within this enclosure, and connected with the palace, were the celebrated *hanging-gardens*. These embraced a square of four hundred feet on each side, (about three acres and a half,) and consisted of ter races supported by walls and piers, and rising one above another, till the highest was on a level with the summit of the walls. The ascent from terrace to terrace was by steps ten feet wide. These terraces were covered with earth, and planted with various flowers, shrubs, and trees; the soil being deep enough to give root even to large trees. Upon the uppermost of these terraces was a reservoir, supplied with water from the river, by means of an engine; and from this reservoir the gardens on the other terraces were irrigated as occasion required. This novel and extraordinary fabric was constructed by Nebuchadnezzar to gratify his wife, who was a native of Media, with something like a resemblance to the hills and woods of her native country. Its summit commanded an extensive prospect of the wide plain of Shinar, and all the splendid monuments of the mighty city; and it was probably from one of its lofty terraces that Nebuchadnezzar, filled with pride and arrogance, was surveying the wonders of his " golden city," exclaiming, " Is not this great Babylon that *I* have built for the house of the kingdom by the might of *my* power, and for the honour of *my* majesty?" when suddenly the boastful monarch, because he gave not God the glory, was reduced to the abject condition of a beast of the field, until he learned " that the MOST

HIGH ruleth in the kingdom of men, and giveth it to whomsoever he will." Daniel iv, 29–37.

But the great wonder of Babylon was the celebrated *temple of Belus*, the god of the Babylonians. It consisted of an enclosure up ward of one thousand feet square, and was surrounded by a wall adorned with several gates of brass. In this area were several sacred buildings; but the most remarkable was a prodigious tower which stood in the centre. It was built in a pyramidal form, consisting of a succession of towers rising one above another, and gradually diminishing in size, till the whole had numbered eight. The base, or lower tower, was more than five hundred feet square, and the height of the whole was also upward of five hundred feet. It was one of the most stupendous edifices ever erected by man, exceeding in height, though smaller at the base, the highest of the Egyptian pyramids:

> "Above the walls high soaring it arose,
> And seem'd to prop the sky."

The ascent to the top was by a path formed on the outside of the towers, and in the middle of the ascent was a resting-place provided with seats. On the summit of the highest tower was a magnificent temple, expressly sacred to Belus, furnished with a splendid couch, near which was a table of gold; but there was no statue, the god being supposed to inhabit it at will.*

The riches and splendour of this temple were immense. When it was plundered by Xerxes, the value of the golden images and sacred utensils which he took from it is said by Diodorus to have amounted to six thousand and thirty Babylonish talents, equal to one hundred millions of dollars. It was in this temple that Nebuchadnezzar deposited the golden vessels which he took from the house of the Lord at Jerusalem, and which were afterward restored to the Jews, on their return from the captivity. 2 Chron. xxxvi, 7; Ezra v, 13, 16.

This celebrated tower is not supposed to have been entirely the work of Nebuchadnezzar. The general opinion, which we see no reason to doubt, is, that the remains of the original tower of Babel formed the nucleus or body of it. It is probable that this unfinished edifice being too massive to be easily removed, Nebuchadnezzar took the idea of rendering this ruin the principal ornament of the city which it was his pride to embellish. What-

* Herodotus.

ever additions he made to it, there is no doubt that its original shape was preserved; for not only would it have taken immense labour and expense to alter it, but the pyramidal form of the temple of Belus, as we have described it from the accounts of ancient writers, "is one which would hardly have been thought of in such comparatively late times as those of Nebuchadnezzar, being in its simplicity and proportions characteristic not only of very ancient, but of the *most* ancient constructed masses which have been known to exist upon earth."*

Of the other public works of the Babylonians, the most remarkable, and at the same time the most useful, were the numerous large canals, and an immense artificial lake of almost incredible dimensions, which were excavated for the purpose of drawing off the waters of the Euphrates, when flooded by the melting of the snows on the mountains of Armenia. "Into this prodigious basin, the overflowings of the rivers were directed by the channel of the canals, during the summer months of the year; and the waters received there were suffered to flow out, as occasion required, for the purpose of irrigating the surrounding country."

" Of the number of inhabitants which Baby-

* Pictorial Bible.

lon contained, ancient writers have left us no account; and, as we observed in our account of Nineveh, the population of ancient cities is not to be estimated by the extent of ground which they occupy. The houses usually stand so much apart, and every respectable house is built with such large open courts, and there are often so many gardens and plantations, that Asiatic towns do not generally contain any thing near so large a population as towns of similar extent with us. How well these remarks will apply to Babylon, will be seen from the express testimony of an ancient writer. "The buildings," says Quintus Cintius, "do not reach to the walls, but are at the distance of an acre from them. Neither is the whole city covered with houses, but only ninety stadia; nor do the houses stand in rows by each other, but the intervals which separate them are sown and cultivated, that they may furnish subsistence in case of siege." Indeed, Babylon might rather be considered as a kind of walled province than a city, in the modern acceptation of the term.

The foregoing particulars will, it is hoped, have assisted the reader in forming some faint idea of the magnitude and magnificence of that mighty city, which was " the beauty of the Chaldees' excellency," and the wonder of the ancient world; in whose courts and palaces Daniel, instructed by prophetic vision, unrolled the volume of futurity, and read the history of time to the consummation of all things; whose streets were so often traversed by the exiles of Zion, when "the Lord in his anger cast down from heaven unto the earth the beauty of Israel;" and whose glory, pride, and desolation are depicted by the Jewish prophets in some of the sublimest strains of Hebrew poetry.

The prophecies respecting Babylon are contained in the books of Isaiah and Jeremiah. They extend through several chapters, but the following passages will be found to embrace their substance. In the extracts from Isaiah we have followed Bishop Lowth's translation:

"THE ORACLE CONCERNING BABYLON, WHICH WAS REVEALED TO ISAIAH THE SON OF AMOZ.

A sound of a multitude in the mountains, as of a great people;
A sound of the tumult of kingdoms, of nations gathered together!
Jehovah, God of hosts, mustereth the host for the battle.
Behold, the day of Jehovah cometh, inexorable;
Even indignation, and burning wrath:
To make the land a desolation;

.And her sinners he shall destroy out of her.
Behold, I raise up against them the Medes ;
Who shall hold silver of no account ;
And as for gold, they shall not delight in it.
Their bows shall dash the young men ;
And on the fruit of the womb they shall have no mercy ;
Their eye shall have no pity, even on the children.
And Babylon shall become, she that was the beauty of
    kingdoms,
The glory of the pride of the Chaldees,
As the overthrow of Sodom and Gomorrah by the hand
    of God.
It shall not be inhabited for ever ;
Neither shall it be dwelt in from generation to genera-
    tion :
Neither shall the Arabian pitch his tent there ;
Neither shall the shepherds make their fold there.
But there shall the wild beasts of the desert lodge ;
And howling monsters shall fill their houses :
And there shall the daughters of the ostrich dwell ;
And there shall the satyrs hold their revels.
And wolves shall howl to one another in their palaces ;
And dragons in their voluptuous pavilions."

Isa. xiii, 3, 4, 9, 17–22.

" For I will rise up against them, saith Jehovah, God of
    hosts :
And I will cut off from Babylon the name and the
    remnant ;
And the son, and the son's son, saith Jehovah.
And I will make it an inheritance for the porcupine,
    and pools of water ;
And I will plunge it in the miry gulf of destruction, saith
    Jehovah, God of hosts."   Isa. xiv, 22, 23.

"Thus saith Jehovah, who establisheth the word of his
    servant;
And accomplisheth the counsel of his messengers:
Who sayeth to the deep, 'Be thou wasted;
And I will make dry thy rivers:'
Who sayeth unto Cyrus, 'Thou art my shepherd!'
And he shall fulfil all my pleasure!
Thus saith Jehovah to his anointed:
To Cyrus, whom I hold fast by the right hand:
That I may subdue nations before him;
And ungird the loins of kings:
That I may open before him the valves;
And the gates shall not be shut.
 I will go before thee;
And make the mountains level:
The valves of brass I will break in sunder,
And the bars of iron will I hew down.
And I will give unto thee the treasures of darkness ·
And the stores deep hidden in secret places.' "

Isa. xliv, 26–28 : xlv, 1–3.

In the following passage, the prophet proceeds to assign the reasons why the judgments
of God were denounced against the Babylonians, viz., their self-sufficiency and pride, and
the severity which they exercised towards the
captive Israelites :—

"I was angry with my people; I profaned my heritage;
And I gave them up into thy hand:
Thou didst not show mercy unto them;
Even upon the aged thou didst greatly aggravate the
    weight of thy yoke.

And thou saidst, 'I shall be a lady for ever:'
Because thou didst not attentively consider these things;
Thou didst not think on what in the end was to befall
thee.
But hear thou this, O thou voluptuous, that sittest in
security;
Thou sayest in thy heart, 'I am, and there is none else;
I shall not sit as a widow; I shall not know the loss of
children.'
Yet these two things shall come upon thee in a moment;
In one day, loss of children and widowhood:
On a sudden shall they come upon thee;
Notwithstanding the multitude of thy sorceries, and the
great strength of thine enchantments.
But thou didst trust in thy wickedness, and saidst,
'None seeth me:'
Thy wisdom and thy knowledge have perverted thy
mind;
So that thou saidst in thy heart, 'I am, and there is
none besides.'
Therefore shall evil come upon thee, which thou shalt
not know how to deprecate;
And mischief shall fall upon thee, which thou shalt not
be able to expiate;
And trouble shall come upon thee suddenly, of which
thou shalt have no apprehension."

Isa. xlvii, 6–11.

About one hundred and twenty years after
the foregoing prophecies were delivered, the
following predictions were uttered by the prophet Jeremiah:—

"THE WORD THAT THE LORD SPAKE AGAINST BABYLON
AND AGAINST THE LAND OF THE CHALDEES, BY JERE-
MIAH THE PROPHET.

Declare ye among the nations, Babylon is taken,
Bel is confounded,
Merodach is broken in pieces.
For, lo, I will cause to come up against Babylon,
An assembly of great nations from the north country:
And they shall set themselves in array against her:
For she hath sinned against the Lord.
Take vengeance upon her;
As she hath done, do unto her.
Cut off the sower from Babylon,
And him that handleth the sickle in the time of harvest
I have laid a snare for thee,
And thou art also taken, O Babylon,
And thou wast not aware.
Cast her up as heaps, and destroy her utterly:
Let nothing of her be left.
The wild beasts of the desert, with the wild beasts of
the islands, shall dwell there,
And the owls shall dwell therein:
And it shall no more be inhabited for ever;
Neither shall it be dwelt in from generation to genera-
tion.
Behold, a great people shall come from the north, and a
great nation;
They shall hold the bow and the lance;
They are cruel, and will not show mercy.
How is the hammer of the whole earth cut asunder and
broken!
How is Babylon become a desolation among nations!"
JER. l. 1, 2, 9, 14, 15, 16, 24, 26, 39, 23.

"O thou that dwellest upon many waters,* abundant in
    treasures,
Thine end is come, and the measure of thy covetous-
    ness.
Behold, I am against thee, O destroying mountain ;
And I will stretch out my hand upon thee,
And roll thee down from the rocks,
And will make thee a burnt mountain.
Set ye up a standard in the land,
Blow the trumpet among the nations,
Call together against her the kingdoms of Ararat,
    Minni, and Ashchenaz ;
Prepare against her the nations with the kings of the
    Medes.
And the land shall tremble and sorrow :
For every purpose of the Lord shall be performed against
    Babylon,
To make the land of Babylon a desolation,
Without an inhabitant.
The mighty men of Babylon have forborne to fight,
They have remained in their holds :
Their might hath failed ;
They became as women.
One post shall run to meet another,
And one messenger to meet another,
To show the king of Babylon that the city is taken at
    one end.
And I will dry up her sea,

---

* The great river Euphrates, the neighbouring lakes and
marshes, with the numerous canals intersecting the country around Babylon, give a peculiar propriety to this allusion to its " many waters."

And make her springs dry.
And Babylon shall become heaps,
A dwelling-place for dragons,
An astonishment and a hissing,
Without an inhabitant.
In their heat I will make their feasts,
And I will make them drunken, that they may rejoice,
And sleep a perpetual sleep,
And not wake, saith the Lord.
How is Babylon become an astonishment among the nations.
Her cities are a desolation,
A dry land, and a wilderness,
A land wherein no man dwelleth.
The broad walls of Babylon shall be utterly broken,
And her high gates shall be burned with fire.

" So Jeremiah wrote in a book all the evil that should come upon Babylon. And Jeremiah said to Seraiah, ' When thou comest to Babylon, and shalt see, and read all these words ; then shalt thou say, *O Lord, thou hast spoken against this place, to cut it off, that none shall remain in it, neither man nor beast, but that it shall be desolate for ever.* And when thou hast made an end of reading this book, thou shalt bind a stone to it, and cast it into the midst of Euphrates ; and thou shalt say, *Thus shall Babylon sink, and shall not rise from the evil that I will bring upon her.*' " Jer. li, 13, &c

At the time when these prophecies were written, Babylon was not a declining, but a growing city. Isaiah prophesied nearly a century before the reign of Nebuchadnezzar, when Babylon was just rising to distinction, every day augmenting its resources and enlarging its dominion; and Jeremiah uttered his predictions shortly before it reached the utmost point of its prosperity, and when human foresight would rather have pronounced its increasing greatness than its utter ruin. Indeed, if there was ever a city whose strength and magnitude appeared to bid defiance to the attacks of enemies or the ravages of time, it was Babylon. Nothing could at that period have been conceived more improbable than that a city of such vast extent, massive fortifications, extensive commerce, and almost boundless dominion, should ever be totally abandoned, and reduced to utter desolation.

But the broad walls and brazen gates of Babylon could not preserve it from that righteous indignation which its abounding iniquities had provoked. In the midst of its prosperity, "perils and great warnings began darkly to environ it." Not only did the prophets thunder the judgment of God against it, but "portentous dreams also visited the sleep of its kings;

and lastly, a supernatural hand wrote characters of fire and wrath upon its walls.—It was at this period, and in fulfilment of the prophecy, that Cyrus broke asunder its gates of brass, and couched himself on the throne of Assyria."

Accounts of the conquest of Babylon are given us by Herodotus and Xenophon, two of the oldest and most authentic of the heathen historians; and their narratives confirm, in the most conclusive manner, the divine authority of the Hebrew prophets. There is scarcely a particular related by the former which is not a striking fulfilment of some prediction that had been uttered by the latter.

Cyrus, who was the conqueror of Babylon, and the deliverer of the Jews, was expressly designated as such, by the prophet Isaiah, more than a hundred years before his birth. See Isa. xliv, 27, 28, and xlv, 1–3, where he is honoured with the appellation of the Lord's " *anointed ;*" and the Lord is said to have "*holden his right hand,*" and to have "*girded him.*"

The prophets mentioned by name not only the principal individual, but also the *nations* by whom the empire of Babylon should be overthrown. " *The Lord hath raised up the spirit of the kings of the Medes; for his device is against Babylon, to destroy it,"* Jer. li, 11. *"Go up, O Elam; besiege, O Media,"* Isa. xxi, 2. "Elam" was the ancient name of Persia, which was so called from Elam the son of Shem, by whose descendants it was originally settled. Babylon, as is well known, was besieged and captured by the united forces of the Medes and Persians, under the command of Cyrus. The king of the Medes at this time was Cyaxares, who is called, in Scripture, Darius the Median. Cyrus was the king of Persia, and nephew of Cyaxares.

It was foreshown that the Medes and Persians should be aided in their undertaking by other nations. *"Blow the trumpet among the nations; call together against her the kingdoms of Ararat, Minni, and Ashchenaz; prepare against her the nations with the kings of the Medes,"* Jer. li, 27, 28. By "Ararat" and "Minni" are meant the Greater and Less Armenia. What nation is intended by "Ashchenaz" is less certain; but it is commonly supposed to mean Phrygia; a conclusion which seems to be favoured' by a passage in Homer, where he speaks of

"The Phrygians from Ascania's distant land."

18

Cyrus had subdued Armenia, Phrygia, and all the other nations of Asia Minor,* before he attempted the siege of Babylon; and these nations were compelled to act as his allies in that expedition. Xenophon expressly mentions the Armenians, Phrygians, Lydians, Cappadocians, &c., as forming part of his army.

It was predicted that the invaders of Babylon should come from the north. "I will cause to come up against Babylon an assembly of great nations *from the north country*," Jer. l, 9. "The spoilers shall come upon her *from the north*," Jer. li, 48. All the countries mentioned in the preceding paragraph lie to the *north* of Babylon.

" *The mighty men of Babylon have foreborne to fight; they have remained in their holds; their might hath failed; they became as women*," Jer. li, 30. When the king of Babylon heard of the approach of Cyrus, he marched out with his army to give him battle; but the " mighty men," who in former years had carried the terror of their arms to distant nations, were overthrown

---

* In the conquest of these countries we see the fulfilment of that prophecy respecting Cyrus, in which it was said that the Lord would *subdue nations before him*. Isa. xlv, 1.

with little difficulty, and driven back into the city. From this time the Babylonians " forbore to fight;" dispirited by their defeat, they ventured not again to try the fortune of arms, but " remained in their holds" during the whole of the time that the city was besieged by the Persians.

The besiegers were unable to draw out the Babylonians to a combat in the open field, and they found it impossible to take by assault a city that was defended by such high and massive walls. They then proposed to blockade the city, and reduce it by famine : but this was soon found to be equally impracticable ; for the inhabitants had provisions stored up in the city sufficient to last for several years, besides what they were able to raise in the fields and gardens that were included within the walls. After a fruitless siege of two years, therefore, Cyrus resolved on attempting to get possession of the city by stratagem ; and in this he succeeded. That the city should be taken in this way, and not by force, was foretold in Jer. l, 24, where it is said, "*I have laid a* SNARE *for thee, and thou art also taken, O Babylon, and thou wast not aware.*"

To understand the method by which Babylon was taken, it should be remembered, that the Euphrates ran through the city, with which it communicated by means of numerous brazen gates; and also that there was in the vicinity an immense artificial lake, which had been constructed for the purpose of receiving the overflowings of the river at the time of its annual inundations. Cyrus, by opening the great dam of the trench which led from the river to the lake, diverted the stream from its proper course, and thus laid the channel, where it went through the city, almost dry. As soon as it was dark, the Persians, dividing themselves into two bodies, went down into the bed of the river, both above and below the city, and marched silently along the bottom till they reached the gates that led into the city, and finding them open, they immediately entered, and took the place by surprise. In this remarkable stratagem, the following predictions respecting the capture of Babylon were literally fulfilled:—"I am the Lord—*that saith to the deep, 'Be dry, and I will dry up thy rivers:'* that saith of Cyrus, 'He shall perform all my pleasure;—and *I will open before him the two-leaved gates; and the gates shall not be shut,'*" Isa. xliv, 27, 28; xlv, 1. It was the invariable custom to close these gates every night; but on this occasion they had been negligently left open. Had not this been the case, Cyrus's stratagem would have availed him nothing; and had the Babylonians been aware at the moment what he was doing, they might not only have saved themselves, but might have caught the Persians in their own snare; for had they shut the gates leading to the river, and ascended the walls which lined its banks, they would have enclosed the besiegers as in a net, and might have poured destruction upon them in a thousand shapes. But the attack was made in a quarter where the Babylonians anticipated no danger; and, in the language of the prophet, *trouble came upon them suddenly, of which they had no apprehension.*

The chief cause of this unparalleled negligence on the part of the Babylonians, was the fact that they were then engaged in the celebration of one of their great annual festivals, and were, according to their usual practice on such occasions, spending the night in revelling and drunkenness; and it was the knowledge of this fact that induced Cyrus to undertake his singularly bold and adventurous expedition. Feeling secure in the protection of their impregnable walls, the entire population of the city had given themselves up to festivity. The king was " drinking wine" with his " thousand lords," and the voice of joy, and the noise of riot resounded through the palace.   But while they were enjoying themselves in careless security, the victorious besiegers entered the city unperceived, and surprised them in the midst of their mirth. " That night was Belshazzar, king of the Chaldeans, slain ;" and the nobles of Babylon passed from the banqueting-house to the grave.*   Thus had the voice of prophecy declared that it should be. " *In their heat I will make their feasts, and I will make them drunken, that they may rejoice, and sleep a perpetual sleep, and not wake, saith the Lord.—And I will make drunk her princes, and her wise men, her captains, and her rulers, and her mighty men : and they shall sleep a perpetual sleep, and not wake,*" Jer. li, 39, 57.

" *One post shall run to meet another, and one messenger to meet another, to show the king of Babylon that his city is taken at one end,*" Jer. li. 31.   The import of this prediction plainly is, that a messenger despatched to the palace from one end of the city with the information that the city was taken at the point from which he started, should there meet another messenger bringing the same intelligence from the opposite quarter.   We have already stated, that

* Read, in connection with the above, the fifth chapter of Daniel.

Cyrus formed his troops into two divisions, one of which entered at each end of the city; and we learn from Herodotus, that owing to the great extent of the city, and the suddenness of the attack, the people in the extreme parts were made prisoners before those in the centre knew any thing of their danger. The first intelligence, therefore, of the capture of the city, that would reach the palace, which stood in the centre, would naturally be communicated by messengers or fugitives from each end.

"*Her young men shall fall in the streets, and all her men of war shall be cut off,*" Jer. 1, 30; "*Every one that is found shall be thrust through,*" Isa. xiii, 15. Such is the prophecy; and what was the fact? Xenophon informs us that Cyrus, after he had taken the city, "sent a body of horse up and down through the streets, bidding them kill those that they found abroad; and ordering some who understood the Syrian language, to proclaim it to those that were in the houses to remain within, and that if any were found abroad they should be killed. These men did accordingly."

The next morning, as soon as it was light, the soldiers who kept the citadel, being apprised of the capture of the city and the death of the king, gave it up without resistance to the conqueror, who immediately placed in it a garrison of his own troops. He then issued a proclamation requiring the Babylonians, on pain of death, to give up all their arms, which they accordingly did. After this he imposed taxes upon them, and distributed their principal houses and palaces as rewards to those whom he considered most deserving among his offi-cers. Thus did Cyrus, almost without any loss on his part, make himself master of the strongest city in the world.

By this blow an end was put to the great As-syrian empire of Babylon, by which so many other empires had been overthrown; and thus, as had been predicted, "*the hammer*" which had broken the nations was at length itself "*cut asunder and broken,*" Jer. l, 23.

The inspired seers declared that Babylon should never recover from its overthrow. "*It shall sink,*" said Jeremiah, "*and shall not rise again,*" Jer. li, 64. The prophet Isaiah, too, in foretelling its ruin, made use of a comparison which precluded all hope of its restoration. "*It shall be,*" said he, "*as when God overthrew Sodom and Gomorrah. It shall never be inhabit-ed, neither shall it be dwelt in from generation to generation,*" Isa. xiii, 19, 20. It was in the last particular—its final and utter desolation—that Babylon was to resemble the " cities of the plain ;" for as to the method and time employed in producing the determined end, there was in the two cases a wide difference. In the one case it was accomplished, as in a moment, by the immediate interposition of Heaven; in the other, human agency was employed to bring about the same end by slow though sure degrees.

The first step in its progress to ruin was its ceasing to be the sole capital of the empire ; the Persian kings preferring to reside the greater part of their time at Susa, [Shushan,] Ecbatana, and Persepolis. This was a great blow to the prosperity and importance of Babylon.

The next step to its desolation was its re bellion against Darius Hystaspes,* which took place about twenty years after its capture by Cyrus. Impatient of their subjection, and relying as heretofore upon the strength of their fortifications, which had been in no wise injured by the conquerors, the Babylonians, after

* This monarch was the third in succession from Cyrus. Cyrus was succeeded by his son Cambyses, and he by a usurper named Smerdis : the former of these is called in Scripture *Ahasuerus*, and the latter, *Artaxerxes*. Ezra iv, 5–24. Darius Hystaspes is the Darius spoken of in the same chapter.

having secretly stored the city with provisions for a siege, broke into open revolt, and defied the whole power of the Persian empire. Darius with his forces marched against the city, and the Babylonians, finding themselves beset with an army which they were unable to withstand in the open field, turned their whole attention to the supporting of themselves during the blockade, trusting that they would be enabled to hold out until Darius, wearied by the length of the siege, and hopeless of taking the city, should give up the attempt in despair. To make their provisions last the longer they determined to put to death all who were unable to assist in the defence of the city; and accordingly they strangled all their wives, sisters, daughters, and young children, except that every man saved from his family one female whom he loved the best. May we not consider this as the fulfilment of that prophecy of Isaiah (xlvii, 9) which declared, that "in one day two things, *loss of children and widowhood*, should come upon them in their perfection?" "For," as Dr. Prideaux observes, "in what greater perfection could these calamities come upon them, than when they themselves, thus upon themselves, became the executioners of them?"

The barbarous policy of the Babylonians, however, availed them nothing; for Darius, after having vainly spent a year and eight months in the siege, at length took the city by the following extraordinary stratagem :—

Zopyrus, one of Darius's most honourable nobles, after having cut off his nose and ears, and mangled his body with stripes, fled in this deplorable condition to the besieged. He represented to the Babylonians that the cruel treatment of which his body bore such indelible marks, had been inflicted upon him by Darius, because he had advised that monarch to give up the siege; and pretended that he was now burning with a desire to revenge himself upon the tyrant. The Babylonians, suspecting nothing, admitted him to their councils and their confidence, and gave him an important military command. After he had successfully attacked, and entirely destroyed three several detachments of the Persian troops, and when it was supposed that his fidelity had been sufficiently proved, he was raised to the chief command of the army, and intrusted with the high and responsible office of guardian of the walls. Darius, as if about to make an assault, then advanced with all his army to the walls; when Zopyrus, as he had designed, opened the gates

to him, and the city was taken without difficul
ty.   The treachery of Zopyrus equally sur
prised the Persians and the Babylonians; for
the whole scheme was preconcerted by him
and Darius, and, until its development, was
unknown to any other person.

As soon as the Persians got possession of
the place, they put three thousand of the principal citizens, who had been most active in the
revolt, to a painful and lingering death.   *They
were cruel, and showed no mercy.* Jer. l, 42.

Darius then took effectual measures to prevent a second insurrection of the inhabitants ;
for he broke down the greater part of the walls,
reducing them to one-fourth of their former
height ; and he also took away the gates.   And
herein commenced the fulfilment of that prophecy of Jeremiah which declared that "*the broad
walls of Babylon should be utterly broken, and her
high gates burned with fire,*"* Jer. li, 58.

After its conquest by Darius, Babylon was
always regarded by the Persian monarchs with

---

* By the prediction that the "gates" should be "burned
with fire," we can understand no more than that they
should be taken away and melted down, that the metal of
which they were composed might be used for some other
purpose ; for being made of solid brass, they could not be
"burned" in the ordinary sense of the word.

a jealous eye. Xerxes, the son and successor of Darius, on his return from his unsuccessful expedition into Greece, passed through Babylon: while there, he laid hands upon the massive golden statue, and other treasures contained in the temple of Belus ; and then commanded that vast and magnificent building to be destroyed. According to Arrian, the other temples in the city also shared the same fate. The value of the images and other plunder taken by Xerxes at this time, amounted, according to the account furnished by Diodorus, to about one hundred millions of dollars. In the pillage and destruction of these temples we see the fulfilment of the following predictions :—"*I will punish Bel in Babylon; I will bring forth out of his mouth that which he had swallowed up; and I will do judgment upon all the graven images of Babylon,*" Jer. li, 44, 47. See also similar predictions in Isa. xxi, 9, and Jer. l, 2.

After Alexander had overthrown the Persians, he advanced to Babylon, which he took without resistance ; for the Persians had been such severe masters to the Babylonians, that the latter hailed with joy the change of rulers, and poured forth in crowds to meet the conqueror. On entering the city, his first care was to restore the shrines that had been destroyed by Xerxes; and he even undertook to rebuild the temple of Belus in all its former magnificence. In this undertaking he was eagerly assisted by all the inhabitants except the Jews, who alone refused to have any thing to do with the work; but the attempt was soon abandoned, for the mass of rubbish under which the remains of the temple lay buried was so immense, that Strabo tells us ten thousand men would have been required to work for two months in only clearing it away. The design of Alexander was to restore Babylon to its ancient glory, and make it the metropolis of his empire, and the central point of the commerce of the world; and, with his characteristic energy, he took measures to carry his plans into effect. But Providence interposed. At the very moment when it seemed as if the declared purpose of Jehovah respecting Babylon was about to be frustrated, Alexander, then in the height of his glory, and the flower of his age, was cut off, and his project perished with him.[*]

Babylon was at this time completely fallen from her ancient splendour, and was beginning to wear a desolate appearance. Seleucus Ni-

---

[*] He died at Babylon, in the year 323 before Christ, and in the thirty-second or thirty-third year of his age.

cator, who succeeded Alexander in this portion of his empire, abandoned Babylon altogether, and transferred the capital of his kingdom to a new city which he had built on the banks of the Tigris, and which he called Seleucia, after his own name. To this place the greater part of the inhabitants of Babylon removed.

From this period Babylon rapidly hastened to that state of utter desolation to which it had been doomed by the word of prophecy. Strabo says,—" None of Alexander's successors ever cared more for Babylon ; and the remains of that city were entirely neglected. The Persians destroyed one part of it, and time, and the indifference of the Macedonian princes, completed its ruin, especially after Seleucus Nicator had built Seleucia in its neighbourhood. And now (he adds) Seleucia is greater than Babylon, which is so much deserted that one may apply to it what the comic poet said of another place,

' The great city is become a great desert.' "

Such was its condition in the time of Strabo, who flourished a few years before the birth of Christ. Pausanias, who lived nearly two hundred years later, says, there was then " nothing remaining but the walls ;" and Lucian, who wrote about the same time, remarks, that "Babylon, like Nineveh, would soon be sought for and not be found."

St. Jerome, in the fourth century, says he was informed, by a certain Elamite brother who came from those parts, that the royal huntings were in Babylon, and that wild beasts of every kind were enclosed within the circuit of its walls, which had been repaired for that purpose. All the space within the walls, he tells us, was a desolation.* Cyril of Alexandria, who died in 444, tells us, that the canals drawn from the Euphrates having filled up, the soil of Babylon had become nothing better than a marsh.

Thus it appears, that in the fifth century after Christ, the purpose of the Lord respecting Babylon, to make it "a desolation without an inhabitant," had been fully accomplished.

The prophets not only foretold the destruction of Babylon, and the circumstances that should lead to it, but also depicted, with singular minuteness and accuracy, the appearance which it would exhibit in its state of desolation; and the wonderful correspondence between their predictions and the narratives of those

* St. Jerome on Isaiah; quoted by Bishop Newton.

travellers who have visited the place, fully establish the divinity of that inspiration under which they wrote and spoke.

"*The broad walls of Babylon shall be utterly broken,—yea, the walls of Babylon shall fall,*" Jer. li, 44, 58. The walls of Babylon are said by Herodotus to have been two hundred cubits, or three hundred and fifty feet high; while Strabo states their height at fifty cubits. They were reduced from the former height to the latter by Darius, (as mentioned in page 284,) and in that circumstance, this prediction was partially fulfilled. Since that time, the words of the prophecy have been accomplished in their fullest signification. "The broad walls of Babylon are *utterly* broken." Among the numerous travellers who have visited the site, some of whom have traversed the ruins for miles, in various directions, and expended days in their search after the walls of Babylon, not one has succeeded in discovering the least vestige of their remains, or any thing to point out the spot on which they stood. One traveller [Capt. Frederick] explored a tract of country twelve miles in width and twenty-one in length, along the Euphrates, examining both banks of the river, and could perceive nothing to indicate that either a wall or a ditch had ever exist-

19

ed within this area. It may at first view excite astonishment that not the slightest traces of these
prodigious walls are now to be seen ; but this astonishment will be somewhat abated when it is
remembered, that for more than two thousand
years the ruins of Babylon have served as
quarries for the construction of new cities.
Nearly all the cities that have arisen in its
neighbourhood within that period have been built
with bricks taken from thence ; and even at
the present day, persons are almost continually engaged in digging into the remaining
mounds of ruins and carrying away the bricks
as fast as they can extract them.

"*Cast her up as heaps, and destroy her utterly,*" Jer. l, 26. "*Babylon shall become heaps,*"
Jer. li, 37. There is no standing ruin of this
primitive and devoted city, but the whole is a
collection of "heaps," which at a distance appear like natural hills, except that no green
thing grows upon them ; but a nearer approach
shows that they are composed of bricks and rubbish, and cover all that remains of "the beauty of
the Chaldee's excellency." "The ruins," says
Mr. Rich, "consist of mounds of earth, formed by
the decomposition of buildings, channelled and
furrowed by the weather, and the surface of
them strewed with pieces of brick, bitumen

and pottery." These heaps or mounds, he tells us, " are of such indeterminate figures, variety, and extent, as to involve in inextricable confusion the person who should have formed any theory respecting them." " Vast *heaps*," says Mr. Keppel, " constitute all that now remains of ancient Babylon." Mr. Ryal says,— " The ruins were visible at some distance, and rose above the plain in several detached and gigantic masses. On a near examination, we found them to consist of a collection of lofty ridges, and some immense *heaps* of pulverized bricks and rubbish, excavated and turned up in every direction." In another place he remarks, —" So complete and signal has been the destruction of Babylon, and so truly have the prophecies concerning her been fulfilled, that the traveller, in contemplating the almost undefinable evidences of her former existence, may look in vain, beyond a few *broken mounds* and *heaps of rubbish*, for more satisfactory proofs to assist him in his researches."* Other travellers also describe the ruins of Babylon as consisting of mere " heaps," "hillocks," "mounds," &c.

* Journal of an excursion to Babylon and the tower of Babel, in 1839. Published in the London Methodist Magazine for June, 1840.

"*And I will make it—pools of water,*" Isa. xiv, 23. The canals and embankments, constructed to preserve the country during annual inundations, being now destroyed, the river overflows unrestrained; "and the floods, in their season, convert the surrounding country into a *morass* of many miles in extent."* "The ruins of Babylon are then inundated so as to render many parts of them inaccessible, by converting the valleys among them into *morasses*."† "For a long time after the general subsiding of the Euphrates, great part of the plain is little better than a *swamp;* and large deposites of water are left stagnant in the hollows between the ruins; again verifying the threat denounced against it."‡

"*It shall never be inhabited, neither shall it be dwelt in from generation to generation,*" Isa. xiii, 20. All writers and travellers agree in declaring that the ruins of Babylon have for ages been wholly forsaken. Fourteen centuries have passed away since they were inhabited by man. Babylon is now "a tenantless and desolate metropolis."§ "The solitude of death reigns where a tumultuous throng once crowded the streets; and the silence of the tomb is substituted for the hum of public places." The

, * Ryal.   † Rich.   ‡ Porter.   § Keppel.

full accomplishment of the prophecy is also certain:—"*Babylon shall be desolate for ever,—it shall never be inhabited;*" its ruins, as we have already described them, being in such a state as to preclude the possibility of their ever being again tenanted by human beings.

"*Neither shall the Arabian pitch tent there; neither shall the shepherds make their folds there,*" Isa. xiii, 20. Not only is Babylon destitute of *settled* inhabitants, but even the wild sons of Ishmael, in their wandering life, refuse to pitch their tents amid its ruins, or to fold their flocks upon its desecrated site. One reason for this is the fact that no pasture is to be found there; "the whole site being a perfect desolation, on which nothing useful to man, or to the beasts for which he cares, can be discovered." Besides this, the Arabs are so firmly convinced that the ruins are haunted by multitudes of evil spirits, that even when employed as guides to travellers, they cannot be induced to remain in the neighbourhood of the principal mounds after night-fall. This superstitious dread would, of itself, prevent the Arabian from pitching his tent there, even if he could find rich pastures for his flock.*

"*But wild beasts of the desert shall lie there;*

* Pictorial Bible—Rich's Memoir—Mignan's Travels.

and their houses shall be full of doleful creatures; and owls shall dwell there, and satyrs* shall dance there," Isa. xiii, 21. The ruins deserted by man are tenanted by the wild beasts of the forest; and the untamed lion is now undisputed sovereign of the once mighty Babylon. When Mr. Porter, with his party, were approaching the principal mound of ruins, (the Birs Nimrood,) they were suddenly startled at beholding several dark objects moving along on its summit. Mr. Porter, having taken out his glass to examine, says,—" I soon distinguished that the cause of our alarm were two or three majestic *lions* taking the air upon the height of the pyramid. Perhaps I had never beheld so sublime a picture presented to the mind as well as to the eye. While we continued slowly to advance, the hallooing of the people made the

---

* " It is rather difficult to define the precise meaning which should here be given to the original word *Sherim*. In its primary sense something hairy or rough is intended, as in Gen. xxvii, 11. In Levit. iv, 24, and xvi, 9, it is applied to the goat; and in Levit. xvii, 7, and 2 Chron. xi, 15, it is applied to objects of idolatrous worship, (perhaps in the form of goats,) and translated 'devils.' Most of the rabbins suppose *demons* to be denoted; and if so, it must be supposed to mean that demons should be reputed to 'dance there,' which is literally true, as we have already stated."—*Pictorial Bible.*

noble beasts gradually change their position, till, in the course of twenty minutes, they totally disappeared. We then rode close up to the ruins. In my progress I stopped several times to look at the broad prints of the feet of the lions, left plainly in the clayey soil; and by the track, I saw that if we had chosen to rouse such royal game we need not go far to find their lair. While thus actually contemplating these savage tenants, wandering amidst the ruins of Babylon, and bedding themselves in the deep cavities of her once magnificent temple, I could not but reflect how faithfully the various prophecies respecting her had been fulfilled, verifying, in fact, the very words of Isaiah,—'Wild beasts of the desert shall lie there.'" In another place he tells us that the caverns "are now the refuge of *jackals and other savage animals.*" Mr. Ryal says,—"The summits and sides of the mounds present innumerable deep pits and excavations, the dens and undisturbed retreats of *wolves, hyenas, jackals, and wild boars.*" Mr. Keppel saw a large animal couched among the ruins; and also, the foot-prints of a *lion* so fresh that the animal must have stolen away on his approach. The entrances to the dens, he tells us, were "strewed with the carcasses and skeletons of animals recently killed;" and his guide informed him, that "the ruins abounded in *lions and other wild beasts.*" Mr. Rich says,—"There are many dens of *wild beasts* in various parts, in one of which I found the bones of sheep and other animals, and perceived a strong smell like that of a lion. I also found quantities of porcupine quills, and in most of the cavities are numbers of *bats* and *owls.*"

The editor of the Pictorial Bible is of opinion that much of what is prophesied in Scripture respecting Babylon, is to be understood as referring to *all* the ancient cities of Babylonia. Speaking of these, he says,—"Most of the sites that we examined were pierced with holes and caverns, the retreats of *wild beasts of the desert*, and *doleful creatures.* In these sites we have seen the footsteps of lions, have observed jackals, and have been apprised of the presence of hyenas, porcupines, lizards, bats, owls, and other fierce and gloomy animals. About the mouths of the caves may be seen the bones of sheep, goats, buffaloes, and even camels; while the intolerable stench from some of the dens, confirmed the evidence which these indications afforded."

"*Cut off the sower from Babylon, and him that handleth the sickle in the time of harvest,*" Jer. l,

16. The walls of Babylon enclosed a considerable portion of country, which was not built upon, but cultivated and ploughed for corn; so that in case of siege it was impossible to starve the inhabitants into a surrender, they being able to support themselves by their internal resources. But now *the sower is cut off from Babylon;* "its ruins, composed of heaps of rubbish impregnated with nitre, cannot be cultivated."* "The soil, for miles around, consists of the grit and clay formed by the decomposition of buildings, and contains no principle friendly to vegetation. Hence the site of Babylon is marked, even in a region generally desolate, by an appearance of utter barrenness and blast, as if from the curse of God; which gives a most intense and mournful corroboration to the denunciations of Scripture prophecy."†

The divine maledictions were pronounced not only against Babylon itself, but also the whole surrounding country. "*I will punish the land of the Chaldeans, and will make it perpetual desolations,*" Jer. xxv, 12. All writers concur in representing this tract of country as being for the most part a desolate waste. "It is," says Mr. Rich, "the most flat, barren,

* Rich.   † Pictorial Bible.

and dreary, that can possibly be imagined."
" The face of the country presents evidences
of having undergone a sad and melancholy
change; immense and stupendous embankments of canals and aqueducts, now choked
up, for miles intersect the plain; undeniable
and existing proofs, that this part of Mesopo-
tamia, *now an uninhabitable desert*, must at one
time have been a highly cultivated and populous region."* The country which Herodotus
declared to be the most fertile he had ever
known, " is now one utter desert, offering
only some patches of cultivation near the few
settlements which it contains."† " Its abundance has vanished as clean away as if ' the
besom of destruction' had swept it from north
to south ; the whole land, to the furthest stretch
of vision, lying a melancholy waste."‡

" *Babylon shall become an astonishment and a
hissing.—Every one that passeth by shall be astonished*," Jer. l, 13 ; li, 37. None can look,
without feelings of mingled awe and astonishment, upon the now silent and solitary waste
which *was* Babylon. " I cannot," observes
one traveller,§ " portray the overpowering sen-
sations of reverential awe that possessed my

* Ryal.　　　† Pictorial Bible.　　　‡ Porter.
§ Capt. Mignan, as quoted by Keith.

mind while contemplating the extent and magnitude of ruin and devastation on every side."
"A more complete picture of desolation," says
Mr. Keppel, "could not well be imagined. The
eye wanders over a barren desert, in which the
ruins are nearly the only indication that it had
ever been inhabited. It is impossible to behold
the scene, and not to be reminded how exactly
the predictions of Isaiah and Jeremiah have
been fulfilled, even in the appearance which
Babylon was doomed to present." Mr. Porter
thus expresses his feelings on approaching its
ruinous site :—" As we crossed a bridge which
led us into these immense tumuli of temples,
palaces, and human habitations of every description, *now buried in shapeless heaps*, and a
silence as profound as the grave, I could not
but feel an indescribable awe in thus passing as it were into the gates of fallen Babylon.
A ride of an hour and a quarter more brought
us to the north-east shore of the Euphrates,
hitherto excluded from our view by the intervention of long and varied lines of ruin,
which now proclaimed to us on every side
that we were, indeed, in the very midst of what
had been Babylon. These consisted of masses
of ancient foundations, more resembling natural
hills in appearance, than mounds covering the

remains of former great and splendid edifices. Chains of these undulating heaps were everywhere visible. The view was particularly solemn. The majestic stream of the Euphrates, wandering in solitude like a pilgrim monarch through the silent ruins of his devastated kingdom, still appeared a noble river, even under all the disadvantages of his desert-tracked course.—But how changed the rest of the scene! These broken hills were once palaces; these long, undulating mounds were streets; this vast solitude was filled with the busy subjects of the proud daughter of the East. Now, wasted with misery, her habitations are not to be found." "*She is become an astonishment and a hissing;*" "*her pomp is brought down to the grave; the worm is spread over her,*" Isa. xiv, 11.

Among the ruins of Babylon there are four, which, on account of their stupendous size, have excited the astonishment of all who have witnessed them. These are severally denominated the Amram Hill, the Kasr, the Mujelibé, and the Birs Nimrood. The following description of them is condensed from the accounts of several travellers.

The ruins of Babylon are, with the exception

of the Birs, almost wholly confined to the eastern side of the river, commencing about two miles above the modern town of Hillah. The first grand mass of ruin which the traveller meets with after leaving Hillah is that called the *Amram Hill.* This mound is nearly triangular in form; its longest side is upward of four thousand feet in length, and its shortest about twenty-five hundred; its height is very irregular, but the most elevated part is about fifty feet above the level of the plain. Its sides are pierced with numerous furrows and ravines, which have been formed by digging into it for the purpose of extracting the bricks. Besides its immense size, this heap offers no peculiarity worthy of notice; being nothing more than a vast and irregular mass, composed of earth mixed with fragments of bricks, broken pottery, mortar, and bitumen, where the foot of the traveller sinks at every step into the loose dust and rubbish. The name of Amram was given to it from an unfounded tradition that a Mohammedan saint of that name was buried there. Its original state or designation, it is now impossible to determine.

From the northern side of this mound, a valley, one thousand six hundred feet in length, covered with tussocks of rank grass, conducts the traveller to the second grand heap of ruins, which is called by the natives *El Kasr*, or the palace, from a not improbable tradition, that it comprises the remains of the ancient residence of the Babylonian kings. This mound is in shape nearly square, and measures about two thousand feet in length and breadth. Its height is about the same as that of the Amram Hill. Vast heaps of rubbish, overtopping each other like the waves of a great sea, intercept the progress of the traveller as he scrambles up its ascent, or wanders over its summit. Every vestige discoverable in it declares it to have been composed of buildings far superior to all others on the eastern side; the bricks in the other mounds being merely sun-dried, while these are of the finest description of furnace-burned brick,* perfectly moulded, and having inscrip-

---

* "We find two kinds of brick in Babylon; the one burned in a kiln, the other dried in the sun. The general size of the kiln-burned brick is thirteen inches square, by three thick. They are of several different colours; the finest are of a whitish yellow, like our fire bricks; the coarsest are red, like our common bricks; and there are some which have a blackish cast, and are very hard. The sun-dried bricks are considerably larger than those baked in the kiln, and in general look like thick, clumsy clods of earth, in which are seen small broken reeds, or chopped straw, used for the obvious purpose of binding them."—*Rich.*

tions on the lower surface; and although they have been continually taken away from this place, as from a great storehouse, for centuries, they still appear to be abundant. The operation of extracting the bricks has greatly disfigured the appearance of the mound, as the workmen in search of them, dig into it in every direction, hollowing out deep ravines and pits, and throwing up the rubbish in heaps on the surface. In some places they have bored into the solid mass, forming winding caverns and subterranean passages. In all these excavations, walls of burned brick, laid in lime mortar of a very good quality, are to be seen; and in addition to the substances generally strewed on the surfaces of all these mounds, we here find fragments of alabaster vessels, fine earthenware, marble, and great quantities of varnished tiles, the glazing and colouring of which are surprisingly fresh. In this mound, too, Mr. Rich found sepulchral urns of earthenware, filled with ashes, with some small fragments of bones in them. Under this mound, a subterranean passage, seven feet in height, has been discovered; it is floored and walled with large bricks, and covered with pieces of sand-stone, a yard thick and several yards long. Near the centre of this mound is a very remarkable ruin, which being uncovered, and in part detached from the rubbish, is visible from a considerable distance; but is so surprisingly fresh in its appearance that it was only after a minute inspection that Mr. Rich was satisfied of its being in reality a Babylonian remain. It consists of several walls and piers, eight feet in thickness, in some

North face of the Kasr.

places ornamented with niches, and in others strengthened by pilasters and buttresses, built of fine burned brick, (still perfectly clean and sharp,) laid in lime cement of such tenacity that it is almost impossible to detach the bricks without breaking them; and yet the layers of cement are not more than the twentieth part of an inch in thickness. On the outside the walls have, in some places, been cleared nearly to the foundations; but the interior is filled with rubbish, in some parts almost to the summit. One portion of the wall has been split into three parts, and overthrown as if by an earthquake. Some detached walls of the same kind, standing at different distances, show that what remains is but a small part of the original fabric. The Kasr is by far the most perfect of all the ruins, and possesses a strong interest, from the probability of its being the sole remains of the magnificent palace in which Nebuchadnezzar reigned and Daniel prophesied, upon whose walls the hand of the Lord inscribed in mystic characters the doom of Babylon, and within whose precincts Cyrus and Alexander entered as conquerors.

A mile to the north of the Kasr, and full five miles distant from Hillah, is the mound of ruins called *Mujelibé*, which signifies " the overturned." It is of an oblong shape, and its height, as well as the measurement of its sides, is very irregular; the northern side measures at the base six hundred feet, the southern six hundred and fifty-seven, the eastern five hundred and eighty-four, and the western four hundred and eight. Mr. Rich, in 1811, estimated the elevation of the highest angle at one hundred and forty-one feet; but Mr. Ryal, in 1839, states, as the result of a trigonometrical survey of the ruins, undertaken by the officers of the British steamer Euphrates, then lying in the Tigris, that the height of the most elevated part of the Mujelibé was not then more than eighty feet. The summit presents a broad, uneven surface, and is covered with heaps of rubbish, in digging into some of which, layers of broken burned brick, cemented with mortar, are discovered, and here and there whole bricks, with inscriptions on them, are found. The mass of the structure is composed of bricks dried in the sun, and mixed with broken straw or reeds in the preparation. The outer edges of the bricks having mouldered away, it is only on a minute inspection that the nature of the materials can be discovered. When viewed from a distance the ruin has more the appearance of a small hill than a building; and the ascent is in some parts so gentle that a person may ride over it. Some human skeletons, enclosed in coffins, have been discovered in this ruin; these, when found, were in a high state of preservation, but crumbled into dust soon after their exposure to the air. The surface of the mound is covered with innumerable fragments of pottery, brick, bitumen, pebbles, vitrified brick, and even shells, bits of glass, and mother-of-pearl. In the sides deep ravines have been sunk by the periodical rains, and there are numerous long narrow cavities or passages, now the resort of wild beasts. This mound, unlike those we have before described, appears to be the remains of a single building, which in its original state must have been one of the most enormous masses of brick-work ever erected by the hand of man. What was the original destination of the Mujelibé, it is now impossible to determine; some suppose it to have been the citadel or fortress which guarded this quarter of the city; others imagine it to be the remains of the celebrated hanging-gardens; while another party have claimed it to be the site of the temple of Belus. The latter distinction is now, however, pretty generally conceded to the ruin called the Birs Nimrood.

On the western side of the river there are no ruins of any consequence except the *Birs Nimrood*, (the tower of Nimrod,) which stands about six miles from the banks; and is about ten miles south-west from the Mujelibé. It is the most interesting and remarkable of all the Babylonian remains, being, both in magnitude and construction, far superior to the Mujelibé. This huge mass of building is of an oblong shape, and at its base measures two thousand two hundred and eighty-six feet in circumference. At the eastern side it is not more than fifty or sixty feet high; but on the western it rises from the plain in a pyramidal form to the elevation of one hundred and ninety-eight feet, and on its summit is a solid pile

of brick, thirty-seven feet high by twenty-eight in breadth, diminishing in thickness to the top, which is broken and irregular, and rent by a large fissure extending through a third of its height; the entire height of the ruin on the western side is therefore two hundred and thirty-five feet. It is principally constructed of furnace-burned bricks, and appears to have been a solid structure built in receding stages; traces of three of these stages are discernible in the mound, and the mass of brick-work on its summit, which Mr. Rich tells us is of the finest masonry, was evidently the facing of a fourth stage. Every one who sees the Birs Nimrood, feels at once that of all masses of ruin found in this region, there is no other which both in form and dimensions so nearly corresponds with the accounts furnished by ancient writers respecting the temple of Belus. That *building*, according to these accounts, consisted of *eight* successive stages rising to the height of five hundred feet; this *ruin* comprises *four* such stages (the latter imperfect) with an elevation of two hundred and thirty-five feet. The temple of Belus, too, is said to have measured five hundred feet on each side at the base, making its circumference two thousand feet; the circumference of the Birs Nimrood is two thousand two hundred and eighty-six feet. The difference between the two is easily accounted for by the enlargement which the base of the ruin has undergone from the fall of the crumbling materials from the summit. We have already suggested* the probable identity of the temple of Belus and the original tower of Babel. If that first building begun by the nations has not altogether vanished from the earth, there can, we think, be little doubt that its remains are to be seen in the Birs Nimrood.

* See page 261.

On the summit of this mound are seen immense unshapen fragments of *molten walls* and vitrified masonry, some of which measured twelve feet in length, and twenty-four in circumference. In most of them the regular lines of cement are perfectly discernible, and so hardened in common with the bricks, that when the masses are struck they ring like glass. They are as hard as granite, and if seen near a factory, might be taken for smelted ore. They bore ample evidence that the pile had been destroyed by fire, and must have been laid waste by a great and most consuming conflagration. The heat of the fire which produced such amazing effects must have burned with the force of the strongest furnace; and from the general appearance of the cleft in the wall, and these vitrified masses, Mr. Porter is of opinion that the catastrophe was produced by lightning from heaven. Ruins occasioned by the explosion of any combustible matter would have exhibited very different appearances.* It cannot now be seen without recollecting the emphatic prophecy of Jeremiah,—"I will roll thee down from the rocks, and will make thee a *burned mountain.*"†

* Rich—Ryal—Mignan—Porter.
† Jeremiah li, 25.

The aspect of the Birs Nimrood is sublime even in its ruins. Towering above the desert, it still rears its shattered summit to the heavens, and seems in the distance like a hill surmounted with a tower. There are no remains in its neighbourhood of sufficient magnitude to detract from its appearance. It stands alone, as it were, in the midst of a solitary waste, "like the awful figure of prophecy herself, pointing to the fulfilment of her own predictions."

BABYLON IS FALLEN! and in her fall has added another to the sad catalogue of those who, hardening themselves against the LORD, have not prospered, (Job ix, 4.) Not one word of the prophecies pronounced against her has failed of its accomplishment. She is become *a desolation and an astonishment;* " a place which the foot of man seldom traverses, which the ' wild beasts of the desert' make their home, and none but the ' doleful creatures' of the earth inhabit." Her proud millions have been " carried away as with a flood ;" and the cry of the jackal, and the screech of the owl alone " scare affrighted silence from the walls " which once resounded with the din of business and the noise of festivity. The " golden city" has ceased; the "beauty of the Chaldees' excellency" is departed;

> "And Babylon that walk'd in pride
> Now sleeps a shapeless ruin."

From this melancholy scene "we may draw a right image of the frailty of man, and the mutability of whatever is worldly; and learn that as there is nothing unchangeable saving God, so nothing is stable but by his grace and protection."*

* Sandys.

CHAPTER X.

THE PROPHECIES CONCERNING TYRE.

Account of Phenicia—Tyre a Phenician city—Its situation, origin, and antiquity—It comprised two cities ; one on an island, and the other on the continent—Its commercial advantages—Its prosperous state in the time of the prophets—Reasons why the judgments of God were denounced against it—Continental Tyre is, according to the prophecy, taken and destroyed by Nebuchadnezzar—The inhabitants escape to the insular town—The prosperity of the Tyrians is restored at the expiration of seventy years—Insular Tyre besieged and taken by Alexander—Particulars of the siege—It again becomes a place of importance—Prediction that Tyre should be converted to the true religion—Fulfilment of this prediction—Prophecies of the utter desolation of Tyre—Fulfilment of these prophecies, according to the testimony of Sandys, Maundrell, Shaw, Volney, Joliffe, Hardy, Robinson, and Olin.

TYRE is a name which revives the grandest recollections. It was the most celebrated city of Phœnicia, and, for a long series of years, the greatest commercial emporium of the world. " To the Christian, its history is especially interesting, from its connection with prophecy, and from the striking eloquence with which inspiration has described the majesty of its brighter days, and the impressive circumstances of its destruction."*

Phœnicia, even in its most flourishing state, was one of the smallest countries of antiquity.

* Hardy.

It comprised that part of the Syrian coast extending from. Tyre to Aradus, (the Arvad of Scripture,) a narrow strip of land about one hundred and twenty miles in length from north to south; and probably nowhere more than eighteen or twenty miles in width. The space between Tyre and Arvad was occupied by several other towns and cities, all of which were distinguished for their arts, manufactures, and commerce. Of these places, the most eminent were Sidon, Sarepta, Beritus, (the modern Beyroot,) Byblus, (the Gebal of Scripture,) and Tripolis. The line of coast, thus studded with flourishing cities, " with its harbours and sea-ports, and the numerous fleets lying within them, must have afforded altogether a spectacle scarcely to be equalled in the world, and must have excited in the stranger who visited them the highest idea of the opulence, the power, and the enterprising spirit of their inhabitants."*

The most ancient of these cities was Sidon which was the foundress of the trade and navigation of the Phœnicians. This city is generally supposed to have received its name from, and to have been founded by, Sidon, who was the eldest son of Canaan, the grandson of

* Heeren.

Noah. Gen. x, 15. But if this city was founded by Sidon, his descendants were driven out by the Phœnicians,* who there laid the foundation of their future greatness and prosperity. Tyre was founded by a colony from Sidon, and is therefore called, in Isaiah xxiii, 12, " the daughter. of Sidon." "Aradus was founded by another colony from Sidon; and Tripolis, as its name imports,† was a common colony of the three cities of Sidon, Tyre, and Aradus."‡

The country of Phœnicia never became, in the strict sense of the term, one state. The larger cities were always, so far as their internal government was concerned, perfectly independent of each other; and, in every period of

---

* The Phœnicians were not Canaanites. Heeren supposes them to have been a part of the Aramenian branch of the family of Shem, (Gen. x, 22,) "who, at an epoch beyond the reach of history, occupied the extensive plains between the Mediterranean Sea and the river Tigris, the most southern point of Arabia and the Caucasian Mountains, and whose common descent is fully proved by the use of one principal language, divided into various dialects." "They [the Phœnicians] were probably not a distinct people, but composed of Syrian tribes who had settled on the coasts: in no ancient writer are they ever found distinguished by name from them."

† Tripolis signifies *the city of three;* being composed of the Greek words τρια, *three,* and πολις, *city.*

‡ Heeren.

their history, they are always spoken of as separate states. Thus, in Jer. xxvii, 3, and in other passages of Scripture, we read of "the king of Sidon," and "the king of Tyre;" and from heathen writers we learn also that Byblus and Aradus had their separate kings. The smaller cities appear to have been dependencies to the larger ones; thus, in 1 Kings xvii, 9, Sarepta is mentioned as belonging to Sidon. But although the cities of Phœnicia were thus independent of each other in their internal government, they seem to have been at the same time united in one confederation, at the head of which originally stood Sidon, and afterward Tyre. That Tyre, during its most flourishing period, was the dominant city of Phœnicia, appears from Ezekiel xxvii, 8–11, where Sidon, Gebal, and Arvath are spoken of as her allies, and as furnishing her with their contingents of mariners and soldiers; and as Sidon, next to Tyre, was the largest, and Arvath was the most distant of the Phœnician cities, it is evident that the supremacy of Tyre must at that time have been acknowledged by them all.

For the convenience of their trade, the Phœnicians planted in every quarter, but especially on the coasts of the Mediterranean, numerous colonies, of which Utica, Cadiz, and Carthage the rival of Rome, were the most distinguished. By means of these settlements they peaceably spread themselves in different parts of the earth; and by their commerce, extending even beyond these, and by their many great inventions and discoveries, particularly that of alphabetical writing, they exercised a vast influence in the civilization of mankind. "No overthrown cities and desolated countries marked their progress; but a long series of flourishing colonies, agriculture and the arts of peace among the formerly rude barbarians, pointed out the victorious career of the merchants of Tyre."*

Tyre was situated on the eastern coast of the Mediterranean, about twenty miles south of Sidon, one hundred north of Jerusalem, and seventy south-west of Damascus. It was comprised within the limits of the Promised Land, and assigned to the tribe of Asher, but it does not appear that the Israelites ever possessed themselves of it.

In Isaiah xxxiii, 12, Tyre is called the "daughter of Sidon," having been founded by a colony from thence. The period of its foundation is, however, uncertain. Josephus states,

* Heeren.

that about two hundred and forty years before the building of Solomon's temple, Sidon being besieged by the Philistines of Askelon, many of the inhabitants escaped thence in their ships, and built Tyre. But Joshua mentions Tyre as a "strong city," more than two hundred years prior to the time spoken of by Josephus. Josh. xix, 29. "Dr. Hales conjectures that Josephus must have written *twelve* hundred and forty, and that the numerical letter, denoting a thousand, had fallen from the text, or had been omitted by the carelessness of a transcriber This amendment would carry back the beginning of Tyre to B. C. 2267, a conclusion which is supported by every appearance of probability. That Tyre possessed a very high antiquity is rendered manifest by several allusions to it in the books of the prophets, as a place which was very old in their time. Isaiah not only describes it as a ' mart of nations,' but, in anticipating its downfall, he exclaims, ' Is this your joyous city, whose antiquity is of ancient days ?' "*

There were, however, two Tyres ; or rather, Tyre itself consisted of two cities, one of which stood on a small, rocky island, about half a mile from the main land, and the other

* Russell's Connection of Sacred and Profane History.

on the opposite shore. Should, therefore, Dr. Hales' proposed emendation of the text of Josephus not be admitted, the discrepancy between the account given by the Jewish historian and that contained in Joshua, may be reconciled by supposing one of these to refer to the town on the island, and the other to that on the continent.

Of the two cities, the one on the rock was certainly the more ancient, as from thence the place derived its name, the word Tyre signifying a *rock*. But though continental Tyre was the last founded, it was, from its more commodious situation, the first to rise to distinction. Insular Tyre, on the contrary, attained but little celebrity until after the destruction of the continental city, which is, therefore, commonly called *old* Tyre.

Tyre, although the "daughter of Sidon," soon eclipsed that city itself in commercial wealth and political importance. Of all ancient cities, Tyre was probably the most favourably situated for maritime commerce. It possessed, at one time, the best harbour on the Mediterranean coast; and was the natural outlet through which the rich productions brought from India by way of Babylon, Palmyra, and Damascus, passed on their way to Europe. Its inhabitants acquired an early pre-eminence in arts, manufactures, and commerce, and were, perhaps, the most industrious and enterprising people the world has yet seen. They pushed their commercial dealings to the extremities of the then known world, and raised their city to a rank in power and opulence before unknown. The three quarters of the world wafted wealth into its port, and people of all languages thronged its streets. No city, before or since, has centred within itself, as Tyre did, the trade of all nations, and held an absolute monopoly, not only of one, but of almost every branch of commerce. For a long period, not a single production of the East passed to the West, or of the West to the East but by the merchants of Tyre; nor for many ages were any ships but those of Tyre daring enough to pass the straits of the Red Sea on the one side, or of the Mediterranean on the other. She claimed the ocean as her peculiar dominion, and styled herself "Queen of the Seas," a title which seemed justly due to her, as she first taught the art of braving its tempests, and navigating its surface. While the mariners of other countries were groping along their coasts, clinging to their landmarks, and frightened at a breeze, the seamen of Tyre feared to undertake no voyage which the state of nautical science at that time rendered practicable. "They carried the art of navigation to the highest point of perfection of which it was then capable. Their numerous fleets were scattered over the Indian and Atlantic Oceans, and the Tyrian pennant waved at the same time on the coasts of Britain and on the shores of Ceylon."*

Such was the flourishing condition of Tyre at the time when the prophets foretold its utter desolation. And these accounts of its riches and greatness are confirmed by the testimony of Scripture. Isaiah calls her

" A mart of nations,
   The crowning city,
   Whose merchants are princes,
   And her traffickers the honourable of the earth."
                                    ISAIAH xxiii, 3, 8.

And Ezekiel says of her,

" O thou that art situate at the entry of the sea,
   Which art a merchant for the people of many isles,
   O Tyrus, thou hast said, ' I am of perfect beauty.'
   Thy borders are in the midst of the seas,
   Thy builders have perfected thy beauty."
                                    EZEK. xxvii, 3, 4.

After thus addressing her, he proceeds to detail, with great minuteness, the nations and

* Heeren.

21 ·

countries with whom she traded, and the various articles with which they supplied her, and for which they received the wares and manufactures of the Tyrians in return.

Riches and magnificence thus flowing in upon the city from every side, the inhabitants became lifted up with pride, and this was one cause of its destruction.

> "Because thou hast said, 'I am a god,
>   I sit in the seat of God in the midst of the seas,'
>   And thine heart is lifted up because of thy riches;
>   Therefore, thus saith the LORD GOD,
>   Behold I will bring strangers upon thee,
>   (The terrible of the nations;)
>   And they shall defile thy brightness,
>   They shall bring thee down to the pit."
>   EZEK. xxviii, 2–8.

> "The Lord of hosts hath purposed it,
>   To stain the pride of all glory,
>   And to bring into contempt all the honourable of the
>   earth."   ISAIAH xxiii, 9.

Another reason for the judgments denounced against them, was their cruelty to the Israelites in selling them into slavery, Joel iii, 5; and Ezekiel begins his prophecy against them with a declaration that it was in consequence of their exultation over the fall of Jerusalem when it was destroyed by Nebuchadnezzar.

> "Because that Tyrus hath said against Jerusalem,
>   'Aha! she is broken that was the gates of the people,

She is turned unto me,
I shall be replenished now she is laid waste ;'
Therefore, thus saith the LORD GOD,
Behold, I am against thee, O Tyrus !
And will cause many nations to come up against thee,
As the sea causeth his waves to come up.
And they shall destroy the walls of Tyrus,
And break down her towers ;
I will also scrape her dust from her,
And make her like the top of a rock.
It shall be a place for the spreading of nets in the midst
of the sea."   EZEKIEL xxvi, 2–5.

This prediction refers to both continental and insular Tyre, and embraces the whole series of events by which that mighty city was reduced to utter desolation : for Tyre was not to be destroyed at once ; " *many* nations" were to come up against it before its final destruction was effected.

To insert in full all the prophecies respecting Tyre would occupy too much space. They are contained in Isaiah xxiii; Amos i, 9, 10; Joel iii, 4–8; Ezekiel xxvi, xxvii, xxviii; and Zech. ix, 3, 4. By a careful collation and comparison of them, we shall find that they embrace the following particulars :—That the city should be taken and destroyed by Nebuchadnezzar, king of Babylon ;—that at the end of seventy years the people should recover their

liberty, and be restored to their gains and merchandize ;—that Tyre should a second time
be taken and destroyed ;—that the inhabitants
should at one period forsake their idols, and become worshippers of the true God ;—and that,
finally, the city should be totally destroyed, and
become a place only for fishers to spread their
nets upon.   We will now proceed to exhibit
the accomplishment of these predictions in the
subsequent history of Tyre.

*The city was to be taken and destroyed by Ne-
buchadnezzar, king of Babylon.*—Enterprise and
industry were not the only virtues of the Tyrians ; they had an undoubted claim to valour of no
common order.   Though possessing scarcely
any territory beyond the walls of their city, yet,
up to the time of Ezekiel, they had maintained
their liberties inviolate, and had never been
conquered by any nation. Salmanaser, king
of Assyria, then the greatest monarch of the
East, after he had subdued the Israelites and
carried the ten tribes into captivity, turned his
arms against Tyre. He first attacked it by sea ;
but the Tyrians having, with only twelve ships,
beaten his fleet of sixty, he would not again
venture to cope with them on that element ; he
therefore turned the war into a siege, and left

an army to blockade the city; but, though they remained before it five years, they were unable to take it. It was about this time that Isaiah foretold the miserable overthrow of Tyre by the Chaldeans, or Babylonians, who were then an insignificant people, subject to the Assyrians. One hundred and twenty years after, Ezekiel expressly declared that it should be destroyed by Nebuchadnezzar, who was then king of Babylon.

> "For thus saith the Lord God,
> Behold, I will bring upon Tyrus
> Nebuchadnezzar, king of Babylon,
> With horses, and with chariots,
> And with horsemen, and companies, and much people.
> And he shall make a fort against thee,
> And cast a mount against thee,
> And lift up the buckler against thee.
> And he shall set engines of war against thy walls,
> And with his axes he shall break down thy towers.
> He shall slay thy people with the sword,
> And thy strong garrisons shall go down to the ground."
>
> EZEK. xxvi, 7–11.

This prediction was delivered soon after the destruction of Jerusalem by the Chaldeans, and about two years after that event Nebuchadnezzar laid siege to Tyre; but such was the strength of the place that it was thirteen years before he was able to take it. In the language of Ezekiel, (xxix, 18,) he " caused his army

to serve a great service against Tyrus: every
head was made bald, and every shoulder was
peeled; yet had he no wages, nor his army, for
Tyrus, for the great service that he had served
against it;" for the inhabitants, when they saw
that the works for carrying on the siege were
perfected, and that the foundations of the walls
were shaken by the battering of the rams, had,
the greater part of them, taken to their ships, and
conveyed themselves, with their most valuable
effects, to the insular town, and to other places
beyond the reach of the conqueror; so that Nebuchadnezzar, when at last he succeeded in
taking the city, found himself no gainer by the
expedition. Irritated by his disappointment, he
wreaked his anger upon the buildings and the
few inhabitants left in them, razing the city to
the ground, and slaying all he found therein.

*At the end of seventy years the people were to
recover their liberty and be restored to their gains
and merchandize.*—The subjection of the Tyrians for the space of seventy years, and the
restoration of their prosperity at the end of that
period, was foretold by Isaiah in the following
words:—

" And it shall come to pass in that day,
    That Tyre shall be forgotten seventy years,

According to the days of one king;
And it shall come to pass after the end of seventy
　　years,
That the Lord will visit Tyre,
And she shall turn to her hire,
And shall commit fornication with all the kingdoms
　　of the world."　　　　　IsAIAH xxiii, 15, 17.

This prediction refers to the interests of the Tyrians and not to the identical city which was destroyed by Nebuchadnezzar; for contineutal Tyre was never rebuilt, the inhabitants who escaped from thence fixing themselves permanently in the insular town, which is the Tyre afterward spoken of in history. But though the Tyrians, by their flight, escaped the destruction meditated against them by Nebuchadnezzar, yet they found it necessary in their new abode to come to terms with the conqueror; and accordingly they became tributary to the Assyrians, and Tyre was governed by magis trates or judges appointed by the king of Babylon.

This state of vassalage was to continue " seventy years, according to the days of one king," that is, of one *kingdom*. " Nebuchadnezzar began his conquests in the first year of his reign; from thence to the taking of Babylon by the Persians, under Cyrus, are seventy years, at which time the nations conquered by Nebuchadnezzar were to be restored to liberty. These seventy years limit the duration of the Babylonish monarchy. Tyre was taken by Nebuchadnezzar about the middle of that period, so did not serve the king of Babylon during the whole of that period, but only for the remaining part of it. This seems to be the meaning of Isaiah—the days allotted to the 'one king,' or kingdom, are seventy years; Tyre, with the rest of the conquered nations, shall continue in a state of subjection to the end of that period. Not from the beginning and through the whole of the period; for, being one of the latest conquests, the duration of that state of subjection in regard to her, was not much more than half of it. 'All these nations,' said Jeremiah, 'shall serve the king of Babylon seventy years,' Jer. xxv, 11. Some of them were conquered sooner, some later; but the end of this period was the common term for the deliverance of them all."*

The Babylonish empire being then subverted, the Tyrians, with some other remote nations, were restored to comparative independence by the Persians. "They seem then to have been allowed the entire management of their own affairs with the only discoverable

* Bishop Lowth.

limitation, that they were required to furnish subsidies and vessels to the Persians when called upon to do so. Accordingly they did render them very valuable assistance in the famous war of Xerxes against the Greeks; and Herodotus particularly mentions the kings of Tyre and Sidon, as present at the council of war held by the Persian monarch."*

Under the Persians, the people of Tyre recovered much of their former wealth and importance,† and their city again became a mart of universal merchandise. When the Jews were rebuilding Jerusalem, the Tyrians furnished workmen and procured the timber for the temple, thus assisting Ezra in the erection of the second temple, as they had formerly assisted Solomon in building the first. Ezra iii, 7.

But with the recovery of its former credit, Tyre at the same time resumed its former vices; and since the people had not profited by the first lesson which God had given them, by the

---

* Pictorial Bible.

† In point of size insular Tyre was far inferior to the old city, the rock upon which it was built being not more than three miles in circumference; upon this confined space, however, a large population existed, as the inhabitants made amends for their want of space by the loftiness of their houses.

hands of the king of Babylon, but still inflated themselves with ideas of their own greatness, a second judgment was pronounced against them.

It was foretold that Tyre should again be taken and destroyed.—We have already observed that the prophecy of Ezekiel refers to the destruction of insular Tyre, as well as of the continental city. This is clear from the following expressions, which can refer only to the city on the island : " the renowned city which was strong in the sea," xxvi, 17 ;—" what city is like unto Tyrus, like the destroyed in the midst of the sea ?" xxvii, 32 ;—" thou hast said, ' I sit in the seat of God, in the midst of the sea,' " xxviii, 2.

But the most direct prophecy respecting insular Tyre, is that of Zechariah, who lived many years after the destruction of old Tyre by Nebuchadnezzar,* and who thus describes the state of the city in his time, and the terrible overthrow which awaited her, and which was accomplished by Alexander, two hundred and forty years after the ruin of the old city.

> " Tyrus did build·herself a strong hold,
>   And heaped up silver as the dust,

* Continental Tyre was destroyed by Nebuchadnezzar in the year 573 B. C. ; and Zechariah's prophecy respecting Tyre is supposed to have been delivered about the year 457 B. C., which would be one hundred and sixteen years after that event.

And fine gold as the mire of the streets.
Behold, the LORD will cast her out,
And he will smite her power in the sea ;
And she shall be devoured with fire."

ZECH. ix, 3, 4.

It was indeed a " strong hold," being surrounded on all sides by the sea, as with a moat and a girdle, and encircled by walls and fortifications of such height and strength as to be scarcely pregnable, even had they been accessible. The citizens were bold, skilful, and amply supplied with arms, engines, and other warlike munitions, and so great were its resources, and such the strength of its position, that it withstood the power of Alexander's arms longer than any other place in the Persian dominions.

The occasion of its being attacked by Alexander was as follows :—After the battle of Issus, Alexander marched with his army along the coast of the Mediterranean, toward Egypt, receiving, as he advanced, the unconditional submission of the various places he visited, until he came to Tyre. But the Tyrians, being more desirous to have peace with him as a friend than willing to submit to him as a master, as he approached the city, merely sent an embassy to him bearing a present to himself and provisions for his troops, and assuring him of their good wishes toward him. Alexander received the ambassadors with honour, and announced to them his intention to visit their city; but the inhabitants, knowing that it would be dangerous to their liberties to suffer the king with his army to enter their city, and imagining it would be more easy to exclude than to expel their royal visiter, refused to admit him, and sent word that they were ready to perform whatever Alexander should command them, but that none, either Grecian or Macedonian, should be allowed to enter their gates.

The haughty spirit of Alexander, flushed with so many victories, was ill able to brook such a reply: in a great fury he commanded the ambassadors who brought it to return, and resolved, at all hazards, to reduce the city to submission. He accordingly made preparations for the attack, while the inhabitants, with equal vigour, prepared for their defence; and "the siege, though it lasted but seven months, was one of the most sanguinary conflicts, on both sides, that the collision of human passions and of human interests ever produced."

" Apparently, no monarch ever undertook a more hopeless task than the capture of Tyre, with the means of offence possessed by Alexander. But no difficulties could daunt him.

Without a single ship, and in the face of a formidable navy, he prepared to take an island fortress with his land forces. His plan was to construct a mound or causeway, from the shore to the city walls, erect his battering-rams on the western end, there effect a breach, and carry the town by storm."*

The arm of the sea which separated the island from the continent was about half a mile wide; near the shore the water was shallow, but as it approached the city the depth increased to about eighteen feet. The causeway was formed by sinking piles into the sea, and filling up the intermediate space with stones and earth. For this purpose abundant materials were found in the ruins of old Tyre, which had lain scattered on the shore for two hundred and forty years; its stones, timber, and even the very rubbish, were collected; not the remnant of a ruin was left. Thus did Alexander complete the fulfilment of Ezekiel's predictions respecting the old city, by laying " her stones, her timber, and her dust in the midst of the water," Ezek. xxvi, 12.

The activity of Alexander, who himself superintended the construction of the mole, was warmly seconded by the zeal of his troops. The work proceeded rapidly at first. The wa-

* Williams's Life of Alexander.

ters were shallow; the loose, sandy soil, easily allowed the piles to be driven through to the solid strata below; and being yet at a distance from the city, the workmen went on without interruption. But as they advanced further from the shore, the difficulties of the undertaking became more apparent, because the sea was deeper, the current more rapid, and the annoyance given by the enemy more effectual. Darts and other missiles, discharged from the top of the walls, reached the work in front, and vessels, fitted out for the purpose, attacked it on both sides, so that the workmen found it difficult to carry on their labours and at the same time defend themselves. Alexander then caused two wooden towers to be erected on the extreme end of the mole, and planted his engines in them. The workmen were thus protected from the darts of the enemy, and not only so, but when the Tyrians attacked them from their ships, they beat them back from these towers.

To counteract these measures, the Tyrians constructed a fire-ship, filled with the most combustible materials, and towed to the mound. They then laid it alongside the towers, and set it on fire; from their ships they also cast darts upon the Macedonians in the towers, so that they could not move to extinguish the fire without the utmost hazard. When the flames had taken effect, a general attack was made by the Tyrian fleet in front and on both sides. The Macedonians, blinded by the smoke, and enveloped in flames, could offer no effectual resistance. The success of the Tyrians was complete. They ascended the mound, destroyed the engines, and directed the progress of the flames. They beat down the facings of the mole, pulled up the stakes, and in a few hours the works of the besiegers were entirely destroyed.

Nothing daunted by this misfortune, Alexander commenced the formation of another mole, much broader and stronger than the former, and also gave orders to his engineers to prepare new engines. Finding, however, that it would be almost impossible to complete the mole, or take the city while the Tyrians continued masters at sea, he went to Sidon and procured a fleet so superior to that of the Tyrians, that the latter, after making two or three attacks, found it safer to keep within their harbours.

The attempts to effect a breach in the walls were no longer liable to be interrupted by the Tyrian navy, but great difficulties still remained; for the besieged, animated by the imminent danger to which they were exposed, invented daily new arts to defend themselves and repulse the enemy. From their commanding position on the walls they could seriously annoy the men who worked the engines. Some they caught with grappling hooks, and dragged within the walls; others they crushed with large stones, or pierced with engine darts. They also filled brazen shields with sand, and heated them till they were red-hot, and then threw the burning sand upon their nearest assailants. There was nothing which the besiegers dreaded more than this, for the hot sand penetrated the chinks of their armour, and made the wearer frantic with pain.

That part of the wall which faced the mole was found to be too solid for the battering-rams to make any considerable impression upon it; the besiegers therefore constructed huge rafts, upon which they placed their battering-rams and other engines, and thus the whole circumference of the walls was exposed to their attacks. It was found, however, that these enormous masses could not approach near enough to allow the engines to be plied with effect, as the outermost foundations of the wall were protected by a breastwork of huge stones, placed there to break the violence of the waves. The Macedonians had, therefore, with great hazard and difficulty, to remove these unwieldy obstacles, and to clear the ground. The vessels employed in this service suffered every species of active annoyance from the Tyrians. Small boats with covered decks slipped under their sterns, and, cutting the cables which held them, sent them adrift. Alexander, seeing this, placed a line of boats with decks similarly covered to repel the Tyrians, and protect his working vessels. But this produced no effect; for the Tyrians, being expert divers, slid secretly out of their boats, and swimming under water, cut the cables close to the anchors. Chain cables were finally substituted, and the work proceeded, till, the huge bank of stones being cleared away, the floats could easily approach the wall.

They first brought the floating engines to bear upon the northern part of the wall; but failing to do any execution there, they moved them round to the southern side, making attempts on different parts of the walls as they passed along, until at length they found a more vulnerable spot, and succeeded in making a small breach; whereupon they immediately mounted the breach by the help of their ladders, and began to storm the place; but the Tyrians, without any difficulty, repulsed them. The third day after this, the sea being perfectly calm, a general assault was made. Two rafts, carrying the most powerful engines and battering-rams, were again brought up to the wall, a great part of which fell at the first shock of the engines. As soon as the breach was wide enough, the besiegers entered the city over the ruins of the wall. In the mean time, the fleet had made two successful attacks from opposite quarters; one part of it had forced an entrance into the northern, and the other into the southern harbour; so that the city was taken on all sides.

The carnage was dreadful; for the Macedonians, exasperated by numerous insults, by the length and obstinacy of the defence, and the serious loss they had suffered, showed no mercy. Eight thousand of the inhabitants were slain: those only who had fled to the temples were spared; the remainder, to the number of thirty thousand, were sold into slavery.[*] Thus, according to the prophecy, were the Tyrians "cast out" of the "strong hold" which they had built for themselves; while "their

* Joel iii, 6–8.

power in the sea" was " smitten" by the loss of their navy.

The foregoing particulars respecting the capture of Tyre have been chiefly gathered from Arrian's History of Alexander's expedition. Quintus Curtius, who has written upon the same subject, but whose history is considered less authentic, adds that the conqueror ordered the city to be set on fire: the conflagration, however, if it took place, must have been but a partial one, for Alexander, when he had " ridded the city of its former inhabitants, repeopled it with colonies drawn from the neighbouring places, and from thence would be esteemed the founder of the city, though in truth he was the cruel destroyer of it."*

Tyre, soon after this, again became a place of importance, and was an object of contention among Alexander's successors ; but it never regained its former greatness ; for, by the building of Alexandria in Egypt, which gradually drew away from Tyre that foreign traffic through which it had enjoyed unexampled prosperity for not less than a thousand years, Alexander did the Tyrians more lasting injury than he had done by the capture of their city.

* Prideaux.

But there is a prophecy respecting Tyre that is of a more pleasing character :—*It was foretold that at one period Tyre should forsake her idols and worship the true God.*—The Psalmist, describing the access of the Gentiles to the kingdom of the Messiah, says,

" The daughter of Tyre shall be there with a gift."

PSALM xlv, 12.

And Isaiah foretels, that

" Her merchandise and her hire shall be holiness to the LORD :
   It shall not be treasured nor laid up ;
   For her merchandise shall be for them that dwell before the LORD,
   To eat sufficiently and for durable clothing."

ISAIAH xxiii, 18.

These predictions evidently indicate a period when " Tyre, converted by the gospel, should no more be a scandal and stumbling-block to nations : should no longer sacrifice her labour to the idolatry of wealth, but to the worship of the Lord, and the comfort of those that serve him."* They began to be accomplished in the days of our Saviour, at which time Tyre was still a populous and flourishing place. When he

* Rollin.

exercised his personal ministry in the land of Judea, " a great multitude of people from the sea-coasts of Tyre and Sidon came to hear him and to be healed of their diseases," Luke vi, 17; see also Matthew xiv, 21-28. When Paul, on his way to Jerusalem, visited Tyre, he found disciples there who were inspired by the Holy Ghost and prophesied, and with them he " tarried seven days." The shores of Tyre had witnessed many splendid spectacles, but none so beautiful as that which they presented upon the apostle's departure: " and the disciples all brought us on our way, with wives and children, till we were out of the city: and we kneeled down on the shore and prayed. And when we had taken our leave one of another, we took ship, and they returned home again," Acts xxi, 5, 6. During the persecutions under Diocletian, the Christians of Tyre witnessed a good confession, and many spirits fled triumphantly from thence to join " the noble army of martyrs." After the storm of persecution was blown over, the Tyrians, under their bishop Paulinus, erected for the worship of God the most magnificent te.nple in all Palestine and Phœnicia, and many other churches were also built there. Eusebius, who flourished in the fourth century, commenting on this prophecy of Isaiah, observes, "It is fulfilled in our time. For since a church of God hath been founded in Tyre, as well as in other nations, many of its goods, gotten by merchandise, are consecrated to the Lord, being offered to his church—for the use of the ministers of the altar or gospel, according to the institution of our Lord, that they who wait at the altar should live of the altar." In like manner, St. Jerome remarks, "We may behold churches in Tyre built to Christ; we may see their riches, that they are not treasured, 'not laid up,' but given to those who 'dwell before the Lord.' For the Lord hath appointed, that they who preach the gospel should live of the gospel." Eusebius gives the following delightful character of the church then in existence: "Comely rites and ceremonies of the church were celebrated; here, with psalmodies and other songs of praise delivered us from above; there, with divine and mystical ministry the secret pledges of the Lord's passion were solemnized; and withal, men and women of every age, with all the might that in them lay, with cheerful mind and will, in prayer and thanksgiving, honoured God, the author of all goodness." At an early period, Tyre was erected into an archbishopric, and had fourteen bishoprics under its jurisdiction; and in this state it continued several years.*

But it was predicted that finally Tyre should be totally destroyed, and become a place only for fishers to spread their nets upon.—About the year 639 Tyre fell into the hands of the Saracens. In 1124, at which time it was still a considerable place, it was taken from them by the Crusaders, who retained it till 1289, when it was taken by the Mamelukes of Egypt, who destroyed both Tyre and Sidon, with some other strong towns, that they might no longer afford any harbour or shelter to the Christians. In 1516 it came into the possession of the Turks. Sandys, who was at Tyre one hundred years subsequent to this, after alluding to its former greatness, adds,—" But this once famous Tyre is now no other than a heap of ruines; yet have they a reverent respect, and doe instruct the pensive beholder by their exemplary frailtie."

Since that period it has been visited by numerous travellers; and the literal fulfilment of the prophecy, which, nearly two thousand years before its complete destruction, had foretold the use that would be made of its site, and the

* Newton—Hardy.

kind of men that would inhabit it, has been confirmed by the testimony of many witnesses:

"I will make her like the top of a rock,
  It shall be a place for the spreading of nets in the midst
    of the sea."

Maundrell, who visited Tyre in 1696, describes it thus: "This city, standing in the sea upon a peninsula,* promises at a distance something very magnificent. But when you come to it, you find no similitude of that glory for which it was so renowned in ancient times. On the north side it has an old Turkish ungarrisoned castle; besides which you see nothing here but a confused Babel of broken walls, pillars, vaults, &c.; there being not so much as one entire house left. Its present inhabitants are only a few poor wretches, harbouring themselves in the vaults, and subsisting chiefly upon *fishing*, who seem to be preserved in this place by divine Providence, as a visible argument how God has fulfilled his word concerning Tyre."

* Tyre was converted into a peninsula by the mound with which Alexander connected it to the main land; for the sea, which usually destroys artificial structures, has not only spared this, but has so enlarged it, by washing up the sand on either side, that it is become a solid isthmus, and none, but those acquainted with its history, would suppose it to be the work of man.

Dr. Shaw, who was there a few years after Maundrell, says,—" Notwithsanding Tyre was the chief maritime power of this country, I could not observe the least token of a harbour that could have been of any extraordinary capacity. In the N. N. E. part of the city were traces of a safe and commodious basin, lying within the walls, but which at the same time is very small, scarce forty yards in diameter. Yet even this port, small as it is at present, is notwithstanding so choked up with sand and rubbish, that the boats of those poor fishermen who now and then visit this once renowned emporium, and dry their nets upon its rocks and ruins, can with great difficulty only be admitted."

But the most striking testimony is that of the infidel Volney, who, in an interesting account of Tyre, after quoting from Ezekiel the description of its ancient glory, and the prediction of its overthrow, adds,—" The vicissitudes of time, or rather the barbarism of the Greek empire, and the Mohammedans, have accomplished the prediction. Instead of the ancient commerce, so active and extensive, *Sour*, [the modern name of Tyre,] reduced to a miserable village, has no other trade than the exportation of a few sacks of corn, and raw cotton, nor any merchant but a single Greek factor in the service of the French of *Saide*, [Sidon,] who scarcely makes sufficient profit to maintain his family." The same writer informs us that "the whole village contains only fifty or sixty poor families, who live but indifferently, on the produce of their little grounds, and a trifling fishery. The houses they occupy are no longer, as in the days of Strabo, edifices of three or four stories high, but wretched huts, ready to crumble to pieces." This was in 1784; since that period, Tyre has somewhat increased, and Mr. Jowett, in 1823, estimated the population at fourteen hundred, and the number of houses at two hundred; most of these, however, consisted of only one or two rooms, and were more like huts than houses. Mr. Joliffe says, "Some miserable cabins, ranged in irregular lines, dignified with the name of streets, and a few buildings of a rather better description, occupied by the officers of government, compose nearly the whole of the town. The noble dust of Alexander, traced by the imagination till found stopping a beer barrel, would scarcely afford a stronger contrast of grandeur and debasement, than Tyre, at the period of being besieged by that conqueror, and the modern town of Tsour, erected on its ashes."

The following description is given by Mr. Hardy, who was there in 1833. He says,— "The island is represented by Pliny as having been four miles in circumference, but the peninsula upon which the present town is situated is of much less extent. It would therefore appear that it is built for the most part upon the mole thrown up by Alexander, including a small portion of the original island. There is thus enough of the rock left in existence for the fishers to spread their nets upon, while the principal area, once mantled with palaces and alive with a busy population, has been swept into " the midst of the water," and can be built no more.* The disappearance of the island has caused the destruction of the harbours; and as all protection to shipping is now taken away, Tyre can never again rise to eminence as the mart of nations. There are still two small rocks in the sea, to which the island probably extended. The present town is walled, and is of very modern date. The space inside is in a great measure open, and the houses are mean; the governor's residence is the only respectable building.—No merchant of the earth now enters the name of

* "I shall bring up the deep upon thee, and great waters shall cover thee," Ezek. xxvi, 19.

Tyre upon his books, and where thousands once assembled in pomp and pride, and there was beauty, and splendour, and dominion, I could discover only a few children amusing themselves at play, and a party of Turks sitting in gravity, and sipping their favourite coffee."

The following is taken from Dr. Robinson :—

"1838, June 24. We spent this day at Tyre. After breakfast I wandered out alone toward the south end of the peninsula, beyond the city, where all is now forsaken and lonely, like the desert. I continued my walk along the whole western and northern shore of the peninsula, musing upon the pomp and glory, the pride and fall, of ancient Tyre. Here was the little isle, once covered by her palaces, and surrounded by her fleets ; where the builders perfected her beauty in the midst of the seas ; where her merchants were princes, and her traffickers the honourable of the earth: but alas ! 'thy riches, and thy fairs, thy merchandise, thy mariners, and thy pilots, thy calkers, and the occupiers of thy merchandise, and all the men of war that were in thee, and in all thy company,'—where are they ? Tyre has indeed become 'like the top of a rock, a place to spread nets upon!' The sole remaining tokens of her more ancient splendour lie strewed beneath the waves in the midst of the sea; and the hovels which now nestle upon a portion of her site, present no contradiction of the dread decree, 'Thou shalt be built no more!'"

Dr. Olin, who visited the East in 1840, says of Tyre, "The present miserable town stands on a small part of the east side of the peninsula —the former island. The site is low, and the houses, from whatever point seen, appear to rise out of the sea. It is a poor-looking place, made up of low, flat-roofed houses, has but little business, and perhaps three or four thousand inhabitants. I walked to the harbour. There were then only four small craft in this little port— rather boats than ships: as many more were drawn ashore for repairs. The water is shoal. Mr. Stukes and I took a small boat to perform the circuit of the old city. It could not come to land, and we were carried on board by the waterman. I do not think there is eight feet water in any part of the harbour. This is the ancient port, and it is still enclosed by the remains of an ancient wall, which formed at the same time the wall of the town. Passing to the outside of this wall, we passed quite round the peninsula to the south side of the isthmus. The massive foundations of the ancient pier rise several feet above the shallow water. The stones of the foundation are very massive. The work consisted of a succession of strong towers, connected by thick walls reaching across the mouth of, or rather forming the harbour. About midway, a passage was left for the ingress and egress of vessels. Parts of this pier have suffered from violent storms, and immense blocks of stone are visible through the transparent water, scattered over the bottom of the sea. At different points along this sea-wall are large numbers of ancient columns and fragments of columns, lying mostly in the water. I counted above fifty of these in one place, many of them of a very large size. We traced the old wall around the western side of the peninsula. The whole line is easily traceable by considerable remains. On the southern end of the peninsula, the remains of the old wall are still more considerable. It was strengthened by towers, distributed at short intervals, of which the massive foundations remain. The massiveness of the stones employed in building the sea-wall is, I think, pretty conclusive evidence that this noble bulwark belongs to the early and prosperous days of Tyrian commerce. The whole peninsula, where not occupied by the houses of the present city, is covered with foundations, broken arches, and heaps of stone and rubbish. The modern village has almost no importance of any kind, and it is only wonderful that three thousand miserable people should have assembled upon this sickly spot, instead of living in the more healthy and pleasant mountain villages. The facility of obtaining building materials from the field of ruins, and some advantages of fishing, were probably the chief inducements for reviving this poor shadow of Tyre.

Of *old* or continental Tyre it was expressly foretold,—" *Thou shalt be no more; though thou be sought for, yet shalt thou never be found again,*" Ezek. xxvi, 21. Its ruins, as we have already shown, were removed by Alexander, and now, not a single vestige of the ancient city appears. The traveller, as he paces along its desolate shore, finds it difficult to realize the fact, that

> "———— once it was the busiest haunt,
> Whither, as to a common centre, flocked
> Strangers, and ships, and merchandise."

"The stirring scenes of a sea-port exhibit a picture of more constant excitement than can ever be presented by any other place. The arrival and discharge of ships; the cries of the captains as they direct the ready mariners; the songs of the boatmen, the dash of the oars, and the roll of the sea; the anxious assemblies of the merchants, either speaking of traffic, or proclaiming their good fortune, or lamenting the loss of some fair ship in a destructive gale; the reckless merriment of the sailors, as they enjoy upon land a little respite from their constant toils :—all these, and a thousand other scenes of noise, and joyousness, and wealth, have been exhibited upon this now deserted shore. They have vanished like the feverish dream of a disturbed sleep."—*Hardy*. Not one sight, not one sound remains to bear witness to its former joyousness and pride.

> "Her renown
> Is pass'd away! her palaces are gone!—
> Her riches, gold and silver, precious stones,
> Fine linen, silk, and costly merchandise,
> All, all have pass'd away!"—ATHERSTONE.

"Who hath taken this counsel against Tyre? The Lord of hosts hath purposed it, to stain the pride of all glory, and to bring into contempt all the honourable of the earth." Isa. xxiii, 8, 9.

THE END.